Building Giants

A Proven System To Transform Your
Workforce Through Effective Training

Katy Caselli, Industrial/Organizational Psychologist

Building Giants Press

Apex, North Carolina

www.BuildingGiants.com

Author photograph by Revolutionary Studios, North Carolina

Cover art and design, Jason Caselli

For My Mother, Evelyn Light Pruitt- My First Teacher

Table of Contents

Preface

As a leader or training professional, do you feel like you are chasing your tail when it comes to getting your team members to learn and use new skills? Does it seem like employees learn more often from mistakes, losses, quality problems, and mix-ups than through training? If so, you are not alone. In spite of the money spent on training ($164.2 million in the year 2013 in the United States alone), researchers are hard pressed to define what has changed as a result. We know that huge amounts of training dollars—estimates range from 60 to 90 percent—are wasted.[1] That's not to mention the ongoing frustration for leaders and training staff who get sluggish results, unmet timelines, and low-level skills and performance. Meanwhile, technology, business methods, and competition add urgent pressure for businesses to keep up. Can these losses be reduced? Yes, they can. The key is to understand the ways in which training typically fails and to avoid those losses with well-timed behaviors and actions on the part of both leaders and learners.

What Is Effective Workforce Training?

"I think you should be more explicit here in step two."

Effective workforce training works as a cycle or pattern. It is not all about the training class. A class can be engaging, have a wonderful instructor, and get very positive feedback, yet still fail to bring the needed changes.

Can you identify training programs in the past that did not have a clear result? Perhaps they didn't seem to correct the root of the problem, or were identified as ineffective. In fact, many leaders have the impression that training rarely works in organizations and is therefore a waste of time and money. It is a destructive cycle: the less clearly training is linked to business success, the more likely training budgets will be cut, training resources reduced, and training dropped from the agenda as a business solution.

This book reveals a simple model that bridges the great divide between scientific research and the hands-on, boots-on-the-ground, product-out-the-door world in which many organizations live and breathe. As you go through the process described in this book, you will recognize the reasons for past failures and collect best practice strategies to prevent the typical loss of training dollars, time and effort in the future.

How This Book Can Help You

This book is written to help industry leaders of all levels understand what it takes to make development plans work, taking their organizations to the next level of skills. Human resources professionals and instructors will also learn to differentiate between training plans that are likely to be a waste and those that can make a measurable impact.

Experts bluntly state that there is a serious gap between the existence and the use of best practices for training. In other words, the scientists know that human resource departments and organizational leaders are only slightly aware of the body of research in HR management, industrial/organizational psychology, and learning theory.[2] The field of learning and development is full of best practices, but only a fraction of them tend to trickle down into organizations for their benefit, resulting in a large gap between science and practice.

One key reason is that the instructors, supervisors, and managers assigned to training projects often have extensive experience in their key niches, such as manufacturing, distribution, or clinical research, but little formal instruction in the science of learning and development. And why would they? Their primary role is to lead a group to meet organizational goals, which may or may not include learning strategies. The opposite of that scenario occurs when professionals hired into training specialist or human resources roles have experience and know-how in training systems and instructional design, but little or no direct experience in the industry. The rare professionals who know the industry inside and out *and* know best practices in the science of human performance improvement are worth their weight in gold for bringing about business improvements through people!

Use this book as a translator to bridge the gap between science and actual practice. It brings to life some of the amazing and effective findings in learning theory, instructional design, training effectiveness, adult learning theory, and human performance improvement. With a low level of jargon and simple, step-by-step, practical advice, this book can help you cause real, positive change for your team members. Many organizations, especially those that are small to medium-sized, do not have dedicated training resources. Others may start out with a dedicated instructor or training coordinator when their workforce is growing. Wherever your company is in its journey, this book can help you to solve basic problems caused by low skills.

A wonderful body of research is out there, which has the secrets to help industrial leaders solve performance problems. Unfortunately, much of it is somewhat incomprehensible, and likely inaccessible to the average leader as well. Consider this excerpt from a journal article on training:

"What variables in the mature and diverse transfer literature have exhibited strong empirical support for influencing transfer outcomes? Where are gaps most pressing across each factor affecting transfer?"[3]

This translates too, roughly, "Why the heck do my employees not do what we teach them to do?!" This book serves to translate this body of knowledge into a simple set of instructions that transform employees into high-performing, learning creatures. When we remove the mystery of how to achieve this transformation, you will be able to apply these tactics to the special performance problems that frustrate you the most. Ultimately, the results will persuade other, high-level leaders to support your efforts even further, turning your workforce into rising giants in performance and giving you superstar status as an effective leader of highly skilled people.

How To Use This Book

You may apply this book to an entire workforce, a team, or individuals within a team. Have in mind a particular team member, group, or business problem that you think can be improved or solved with training. As you make your way through this book, you will learn a four-step process:

• Identify the skills and knowledge that are truly needed.
• Design a training intervention to address that need.
• Plan for the use of the training in the job.
• Monitor the use of training to assess if it fixed the problem.

To get the most out of this book, treat it like a workshop. Take a look now at the downloadable document at www.BuildingGiants.com. Download the training plan form in the "book-building giants/training plan" tab. Keep it nearby while you are reading, and for each chapter, note down your discoveries and ideas. By the time you finish this book, you will have a plan for an effective training intervention and a way to evaluate and report the results.

To spark some ideas, consider these questions:

• Have you been challenged to get more from your team?

• Do you have a large organizational change coming that will require significant skills upgrades and behavior changes?

• Are you facing tight deadlines, high stakes, and plenty of pressure?

• Are rework and quality complaints sapping energy and taking satisfaction away from yourself and your team?

•Have you ever wondered whether a particular team member brings enough back to the company to justify his or her paycheck?

• Have you ever hoped that training would alter behavior but not seen much change to justify more?

By following the simple steps in this book, you can successfully meet skill challenges with training interventions. Let's put an end to the "mystery" of losses in training so that you, as a leader or trainer, can see the whole picture of human performance improvement through effective training and development.

Chapter 1: Failures in Training Can Hurt Your Business

Introduction

Let's say "Sue," a longtime employee, has a skill problem. After a new system was implemented to track inventory, other team members used the technology to get through the transition and meet project deadlines. These go-getters were the super users and were selected do the complex tasks in the system. But Sue, in her comfort zone, busily filled the transition time with parts of the job that did not involve the new technology. As time passed, others got the work done and increased their skills due to their familiarity with the new system. When a new leader came along and assessed the team, it was evident that the super users were doing the entire range of tasks the job requires, while Sue was performing a very limited number of tasks.

What factors took this situation into a downward spiral? Fault might be assigned to the past leader, the employee, the training during the transition, or even the design of the new system. Perhaps change management principles were not properly applied, or the training was not adequate for Sue's needs. Maybe the past leader was not attuned to her difficulty in learning and did not notice until the training period was over. Time was allowed to ease Sue into the use of the system, but the rest of the team filled the gaps to get the critical work done. And so the result is an employee whose skills are obsolete and less productive, and no easy solution is in sight.[1]

This Chapter Will Help You:

• Identify losses in training
• Analyze the results of any recent training initiative
• Develop a "prove it" mindset about training

People Are Assets

A typical asset in a company, such as a freezer unit, air compressor, forklift, cryogenic freezer, inventory system, or computer, gets regular attention. It is purchased, set up, tested, and evaluated. It is put on a maintenance schedule and may get additional attention with repairs, upgrades, and assessments.

People must be seen as assets as well. If they are not performing at the expected level, they may very likely be causing the company to lose money instead of make money.

Suppose your team includes a mechanic whose role is simply to make repairs. What is the average amount of time this employee spends on each repair? Is it longer than expected? Does the employee often call on another busy team member to lend a hand?

How often does the leader need to step in to resolve low-level problems? Based on these factors, is this person making money for the company or losing money by taking additional time and resources from other urgent problems in the plant?

The skills gap is often a big drain on profitability for employers. It is often hard to measure, lending an air of mystery to performance issues and invisibility to everyday losses. If you were to ask yourself, "Is my team a high-performing team?" you might have trouble answering the question or defining what high performance looks like.

Typical Losses of Ineffective Training

When training fails to deliver results, what are the typical losses? The following case study described by Edward Shaw illustrates a typical waste of training dollars:

"A few years ago I was peripherally involved in a project in which a large automaker spent millions of dollars on a national training program for worker safety and accident prevention. Not until the money was gone did the company figure out that the injuries the program was aimed at preventing were occurring not because the workers didn't know how to work safely, but because they chose not to. The reason they chose not to was, predictably, because there were

subtle rewards built into the system that served as incentives for unsafe work practices."

Shaw also writes, "As much as half of the gargantuan expenditure [on training programs] is being utterly wasted— squandered on training that's unnecessary, training that is aimed at non-training problems, and training that's doomed to fail by poor design." These are some pretty harsh words, but they certainly have merit. The effectiveness of training efforts has been a focus of human performance research for years, and the results do not look good.[2]

When employees are sent to unneeded training classes, several resources are wasted. Time is one of the biggest losses. While trainees are in class, their duties are not being performed, even though their salaries and benefits are being paid. This situation can overtax remaining employees, contribute to lost productivity and possibly anger customers who receive late orders.

If employees view the training as unnecessary, they will have no faith in it and no intention of using it. Some may enjoy the time spent in the more "relaxing" environment of the classroom, while others may be impatient to get back to their projects. In either case, they are not focused on the training itself.

Even when they do take training seriously, its effects may not last. In the case of safety training, for example, some participants may take the warnings to heart, worry about accidents, and resolve to change their attitude about safety for the sake of their families. However, that resolve may fade in a culture of shortcuts and permissiveness about unsafe habits.

Leaders become impatient with "mandatory" training that erodes productivity and does not return any obvious change to their business area. Training that does not meet the mark can simply waste time, measured in salaries. For example, if thirty participants go to an all-day training and their average salary is $50,000, the waste for a single day amounts to $5,770. Be sure to add the cost of food, since participants in mandatory training expect nice catering. If an internal subject matter expert is assigned to be the instructor, it will take that person several hours to prepare a single hour of instruction. Let's guess it will take twenty hours to prepare and instruct and assume the expert has a $75,000 salary. That's $720.00. It gets much pricier for external instructors, polished materials, and travel for trainees or instructors. But let's just stop there, as you surely get the picture.

Another form of waste is loss of morale on the part of trainees and even leaders. At the coffee table at break time, you can hear trainees mutter, "They must think we're stupid" and "What a waste of time." Adult learners often become impatient when they are not getting much out of a class. Their attitude can translate to hushed complaints, quiet games of hangman, and under-the-table texting.

By now you may be thinking, "Well, training really can't help me be a superstar leader. It won't let me show off my skills in developing a high-performing organization. Why waste my time reading about training, when I should be watching and directing and scolding and generally saving the department from their mistakes?" Before you think too negatively about training, read on for stories that do show a successful outcome, sometimes fantastically so.

For example, the Association for Training and Development (ATD), found that organizations that invested the most in training and development saw a 36.9 percent total shareholder return over three years, compared to a 25.5% return for the S&P 500 index for the same period.) In fact, leaders who demonstrate their interest in team members' development tend to have more engaged and committed teams, reducing turnover and absenteeism.[2]

In this chapter we will read how training, set up and executed following a simple process, shows a fantastic return on investment and solves significant business problems. In Chapter 2, we will stop wasting training dollars by determining if missing skills and knowledge are at the root of the problem. In Chapter 3 we will see how structured training systems can reduce new hire training time by 2/3^{rds} and how one company reduced overall training costs by 50%. And you will read a story of a typical but woefully wasteful effort in training. In Chapter 4, read about a major reorganization and housekeeping effort in a specific manufacturing area (6S). Discover how the training was designed for action and sustainability to support this critical business initiative. In Chapter 5, you will learn strategies to hold students accountable for learning and improving performance. And in the last chapter, read about a leader who was promoted twice in the two years after turning around performance in a large team by focusing on training.

When a bit of science is applied at the right time, leaders do become outstanding through the development of their people. Imagine turning your team into high-performing, competent, troubleshooting geniuses that you can depend on! Imagine blowing the socks off your top leaders by solving nagging, irritating, and recurring problems through effective training.

Evaluating the Effectiveness of Training

Training is identified as a solution in meeting rooms across the world every day. Unfortunately, organizations put faith in the expertise of the instructors and cross their fingers. When training does not bring the expected results, then those fingers might start pointing at others: the learners, the materials, the timing of the training, the instructor, the project lead, and don't forget the human resources department.

Faith in training erodes when results are difficult to measure or are not immediately visible after a training program. But as we will see, training evaluation and analysis of effectiveness are crucial tools to understand and apply. Training does work and will gain support in organizations when it is planned for and evaluated.

A quick explanation of how to define training effectiveness starts with Donald Kirkpatrick and his PhD dissertation in 1959. His method has since been revamped and improved by Jack Philips and Ron Stone in 2002.[3]

Dr. Kirkpatrick's framework is an excellent tool because it explains the usefulness of training in ways that both experts and non-experts in the training field can understand and use. Since gaining a foothold, his research and explanation has given training professionals and leaders tools to translate training outcomes to business outcomes. After reading the brief explanations and examples that follow, you will have a better perspective of how to see training in the future, including its effect and value for an organization.

Level one of Kirkpatrick's framework asks the question: How did learners react to the class? This is generally measured by what we call a "smile sheet," with questions that typically look something like this:

Please rate the following from 5 to 1 (5 is strongly agree, 1 is strongly disagree).

The presenter was well prepared and organized.　　5 4 3 2 1

The presenter covered information in a logical manner. 5 4 3 2 1

The information could be seen and heard clearly.　　5 4 3 2 1

My questions were answered adequately.　　N/A 5 4 3 2 1

(See a full version in the Appendix, and download a copy at www.BuildingGiants.Com).

This first level of evaluation gives instructors valuable feedback on the class design and their presentation skills. The information is also valuable for leaders and training professionals; a positive reaction is a good indication that training was well received. However, it does not predict whether the training will ultimately help the business. (Sorry, it is just not quite that easy!)

Level two asks the question: Did learners master the skills and knowledge presented during training? This is key information, and it is not terribly hard to get. The instructor can use various measurements, such as success in class activities and scores on a written assessment, to evaluate whether trainees have learned the materials or otherwise met the objectives of the class. (Measurement tools will be discussed in more detail in Chapter 3.) If participants can show success at this level, then it should be possible for the needed changes to the business to actually come about. Unfortunately, many organizations stop at the smile sheet and simply report that the class was rated positively or negatively. Objective evaluations give instructors and leaders more to work with by providing evidence that the concepts were learned.

Level three is more difficult for companies, but not impossible. It involves following the trainees out of the classroom to find out whether, and to what extent, they are using new knowledge and skills in the real work setting. Few organizations evaluate training to this level because monitoring people, often by direct observation, takes time and knowledgeable resources. For example, after one training class, I stood at a window with a checklist, watching employees add additional layers of sterile clothing and respirators in preparation to enter a cleanroom. They had to perform the twenty steps in perfect order, three times each, before they were qualified to enter without observation. After several days, only eight of twelve employees had followed the steps perfectly and made it in. It was a very long week for trainers and trainees alike, but this method of direct observation was very satisfactory to the regulatory agencies, since it provided rigorous evidence that the training was effective.

Level four asks the question: Did the training program do any good for the business? Top organizational leaders should ask this question a few months after the conclusion of any training. The goal is to find out not only, which training initiatives contributed to business success, but also why others failed. Yet most organizations do not invest the resources and time to go this far in training evaluation, because results of training are often hard to see, measure, recognize, and report. It takes a bit of planning and foresight to get the information, but it is crucial to do so, especially in high-stakes, highly visible initiatives. Assessing whether the training helped the business establishes credibility for learning as a business solution. If top leaders do not know what training is doing for their business, then budgets for training are limited or cut, and employees as assets go undeveloped, contributing to turnover, obsolete skills, and a general loss of competitiveness.

If you think ahead, you can set up some simple evaluation measures ahead of time. For example, each month a team of five was taking about two hours to export data from inventory systems, rearrange the data in Microsoft Excel, and chart it into reports. After training that was specifically targeted to reduce this time, the team members were observed preparing reports in about forty-five minutes. That's a savings of 1.25 hours per employee per month, a visible and measurable change to the business. At the end of this chapter you will find two additional examples, one that plucks some costly "low-hanging fruit" and another that is a bit more complex, to help you fully understand the importance of evaluation.

Another important level of training evaluation is the calculation of ROI, or return on investment. Jack Philips and Ron Stone[4] developed and explained a method to measure the dollar value of training. Measuring the return on investment and presenting it with credible and inarguable numbers can get quite a bit of favorable attention from top leaders. Reporting ROI requires good data tracking, both before training and afterwards. For example, if the business problem is a high number of defective parts due to imprecise machine adjustments, how much money did the loss amount to monthly? A few months after training, has the problem been reduced? How much is this worth? Imagine the pride when you can show credibly that you removed a $40,000 headache for the company through a training intervention—or even better, a $400,000 problem.

Case Study: Heat Treatment

Let's turn to some "good news" examples of training interventions that returned favorable results. This first case study shows how a very simple and quickly applied training intervention saved a business a significant amount of money.[5]

The heat treatment department of this heavy manufacturing firm was in charge of sending parts through a special furnace in order to harden the metal. Metal hardening required furnace operators to carefully monitor instruments and readings throughout the heat-treat cycle. One such instrument was a probe used to monitor carbon dioxide levels during the heat treat. When faced with oddly fluctuating readings, operators would remove the probe, tap it against the outside of the metal furnace, and reinsert it.

The new manager of the area observed this behavior and looked into the situation. It turned out that the probe, a very delicate and expensive instrument with glass internal parts, had been replaced nine times the previous year and ten times the year before that. In fact, when speaking with the manager over the phone, the vendor of this part expressed concern. The probes should need replacement only once per year. So in all, the company was losing about $22,000 per year in replaced probes.

The manager asked the workers about the practice. The reply was that "it's the way we've always done it" and that tapping the probe was the only way to clear the erratic readings.

The new manager was a subject matter expert in heat treatment best practices, and now he had all the information he needed. He conferred with the learning and development manager, and they put together a training plan.

First they set the following learning objectives:

1. Discover the impact of vibrations on the workings of the heat treat furnace. (Vibrations contributed to probe misalignment, causing fluctuations in readings.)

2. Describe the inner structure and mechanisms of the probe.

3. Use a standard approach to remove, handle, and reseat the probe when needed.

The training consisted of a fun class in which operators were evaluated on their care in handling the probe (which led to plenty of kidding around). After the training, the team as a whole monitored the health of the equipment and watched each other's technique. Over the course of the year, they proudly reported purchasing only one probe, the required and scheduled replacement. The cost of the hour-long class for the six team members, led by the manager, was about two hundred dollars in salary costs, but the saving on CO_2

probes for that year reached $22,000, based on past history. This was an easy training win, and the case study reached the top level of management as an early achievement for the new manager. Since the cost of the training was low, and consisted of salary and instructional prep time (let's estimate 800.00 for a 1 hour class) here is an analysis of the return on investment.

$$\frac{\$22,000-\$800.00}{\$800.00} = 26.5 \times 100\,\% = 2,650\% \ \text{ROI}$$

Case Study: Automated Machines

This case study involves a problem that was not quite as easy, but again was evaluated in terms of the return on investment.[6] The maintenance team of a major automotive supplier was unable to troubleshoot a type of automatic welding machine. These machines were relatively new to the site (less than 2 years). The plant was experiencing a bottleneck in the area of this welding process, and operations were plagued with losses. The number one business impact with the welding machines was downtime. Typically, after excessive downtime a call would be placed to the vendor, who would send a technician to solve the problem at $6,000 per visit.

The operations leadership team was upset over the continued, costly bottlenecks at that step in the process. The maintenance team was also frustrated and under pressure. The vendor was in the business of sales and set-ups and did not like to come out for repairs; their response time and willingness to help seemed to be flagging.

The learning and development manager was approached by the maintenance manager for help with the problem. After a brief meeting in the hallway, they set aside time to delve into the problem with a more in-depth needs assessment.

The learning and development manager started by asking the maintenance team and maintenance manager about the impacts that the business was facing because of this situation. They identified lost production time and the $6,000 cost of each vendor visit. Unfortunately, no records were present to show how much overall loss had occurred during the previous year.

Further questions established the skills and knowledge gaps of the mechanics assigned to repair and maintain the welder. They could do some of the basics, such as setting and adjusting parameters. When something went wrong, they were nearly helpless in identifying and resolving most machine faults. A clear training gap existed. All parties agreed to this and identified specific adjustments and faults the mechanics could not perform.

Next, the learning and development manager called the vendor and laid out the need. For a $6,000 visit, would they teach the basics and effective resolution of faults in order to reduce downtime and calls to the vendor for repairs? To the company's relief, they would. In addition, the vendor created a custom hands-on class, with paper and pencil tests and actual faults to resolve on the units. Each trainee passed the tests at one hundred percent and gave resounding praise for the class and instructor. So far, so good—the participants liked the class and learned the missing skills.

The next step was to watch and wait. The maintenance manager was asked to write down each breakdown involving these welder machines and the time it took to resolve it. He was also asked to make a judgment call of how much downtime and how many vendor visits the company would have experienced with the previous skill level, based on the severity of each incident.

In the maintenance manager's estimation, within ninety days the company averted three calls to the vendor for repairs and reprogramming (at $6,000 each visit), as well as downtime and crushed parts, amounting to an estimated total of $30,000. With the cost of the training at $6,000, the result was an approximate 400 percent return on investment over ninety days.

$$\frac{\$30,000 - \$6,000.00}{\$6,000.00} \times 100\% = 400\% \text{ ROI}$$

The mechanics who went through the training stayed in the job at least an additional four years, and the welder machines dropped off the list of the hottest site problems three months after the training, a very happy ending for operations.

Incidentally, these two case studies were later shared with leaders in the organization who asked for training interventions. The stories helped to change the organization by showing credibility for training. They also showed that a partnership was possible between business leaders and training staff, and that the training department was there to help with business problems, not just to force employees to attend yet another "preventing harassment" class. Showing the leaders how training can remove critical obstacles deepened the organization's learning culture, which helped keep training on the agenda (more on this in Chapter 6). Sharing case studies with leaders also set up a clear model for communicating about problems and training needs. Instead of taking orders for classes in the hallway, savvy learning and development professionals now ask the questions that determine how best to proceed with the performance problem.

These case studies had certain elements behind the scenes that made them successful. Let's define the behind-the-scenes work that brings the impactful results that organizations need to thrive.

A Four-Step Model for Success

How would you like to shine like a hero in your organization for correcting significant problems, raising the bar on performance, and getting results your higher-ups never expected to see? You can accomplish that by following a standard approach to training that works.

In this book, we will explore four basic steps that have equal value in the effort of making training count:

1. Determine the exact gaps in skills and knowledge that are contributing to the business problem.

2. Design an engaging and effective training class.

3. Require and support the trainees to use the skills on the job and change their behavior.

4. Evaluate whether the training was effective (at the individual, team, or organization level) and determine whether the need went away.

A Standard Approach to Effective Training

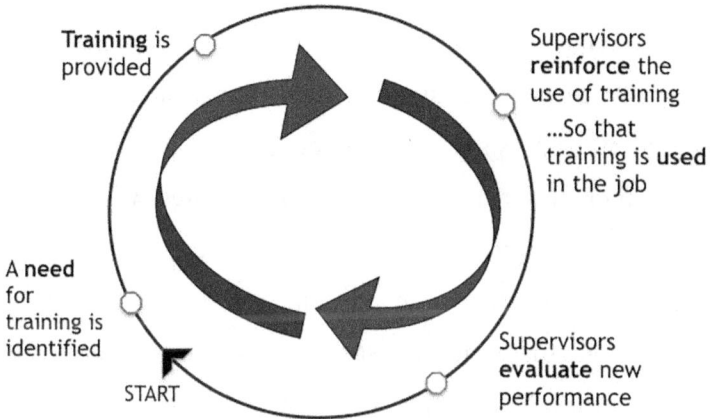

Training is
provided

Supervisors
reinforce the
use of training

...So that
training is **used**
in the job

A **need**
for
training is
identified

START

Supervisors
evaluate new
performance

This diagram is designed to help leaders and training professionals understand this approach. Start at the arrow in the outer circle and go around to the left. Each element is equally important.

Does each element have to be followed exactly? No, you can see positive effects of training without all details being perfect. In fact, most methods presented in books and seminars about developing employees paint a rosy picture that just does not reflect the reality of the world in many organizations. Obstacles will come up, complexity is common, and priorities will shift rapidly. But the more of these steps that leaders, training professionals, and human resources professionals follow, the easier it will be to see results.

Studying the diagram can help leaders pinpoint why some training initiatives do not succeed. A training program can fail at any of the four steps. In some cases, employees go to a class they do not need; in others, the training itself is not designed well enough to be effective and engaging. You might guess that the hardest part is transferring skills from the classroom to the job. But in reality, *all* elements in the diagram have something to do with the transfer of skills to the job. This shows that training works only as a process, not an event.

Read on to understand what, specifically, you need to do to make this four-step process increase skills and knowledge in your workforce. The practical steps in the next four chapters will provide discussion, examples, and step-by-step instructions to make training count, resulting in real and measurable change for your organization. In the next chapter, let's jump in by determining whether there is a training problem and defining the issues.

Chapter 2: Let's Identify the Need

A Standard Approach to Effective Training

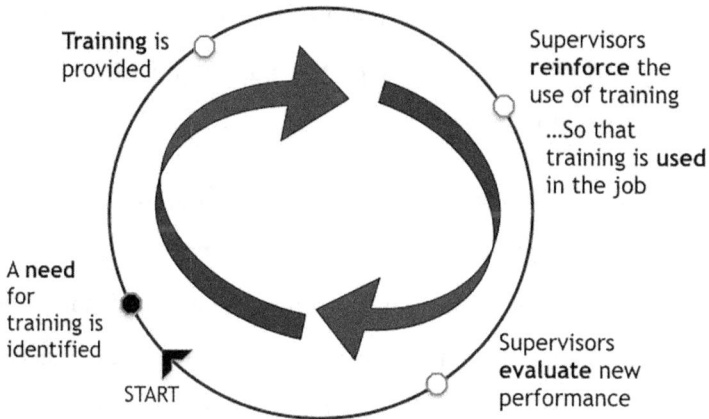

Training is provided

Supervisors **reinforce** the use of training

...So that training is **used** in the job

A **need** for training is identified

Supervisors **evaluate** new performance

START

Introduction

Suppose a problem is identified in an organization. Slightly damaged product is rolling off the production line, causing customer complaints and lost orders. Leaders decide this issue can be solved through training. Employees are sent to the classroom to go over dry, detailed standard procedures and are told to pay closer attention in order to catch defects and run the equipment more smoothly.

After training, the quality problems continue with the same number of defects. Finally the engineering team is assigned to look into the problem. After taking the equipment apart, they conclude the root cause is a slightly warped part that damaged the product just after the operator last handled it. The remedy is a quick replacement part and a check of the part in all future scheduled preventive maintenance.

The loss from this training can be estimated by adding up the cost of time that was wasted, the time and cost of developing and printing training materials, and any money spent on facilities, and refreshments. Also, remember to count up the losses due to work left undone. Not as easily quantifiable is the morale-sinking conclusion that the defects were the work team's fault and that training should be the first fix. If the team had a long record of successfully following procedures and catching defects, then the assessment probably should not have started with training.[1]

This Chapter Will Help You:

- Assess individuals, teams, and the workforce for skill and knowledge gaps.
- Recognize problems not related to skills and knowledge.
- Find opportunities to develop "superpowers" among your workforce.

- Plan for effective orientation and onboarding for new hires.

An effective needs assessment pins the tail on the problem in measurable, actionable ways. Have you ever sent an employee to a training class and later heard the feedback, "It was too basic for me, I didn't really get anything out of it"? Or how about this one? "It was over my head, full of jargon I didn't understand." These situations are frustrating and generally lead to the question, "What went wrong?" It takes work to identify objectives that are a match for the actual training need. Many business leaders turn to training as a solution, hoping it will help but without a firm grasp of how. Let's look at a few ways to ensure a true analysis of the need. We will look at strategies for identifying the needs of the entire workforce, a specific team, or an individual. In all three instances, the approach should be in the form of a question: If there is a performance problem, what is the cause? Is it a lack of skills and knowledge, or is it some other behavior, oversight, or process-related issue?

Assessing Workforce Needs

When assessing needs from a workforce perspective, begin by naming the business problem in a specific, clear way. It could be lost customers, pallets of components not in the correct warehouse location, rework, poor written communication, inability to do accurate forecasting, leaders not using coaching behaviors, employee turnover rates, ladder injuries, or repeated mechanical

31

failures. Think of loss in terms of profitability, customer base, market share, increased turnover, lack of agility in response to business change, or the need to quickly adopt increased automation.

Next, identify the factors that contribute to the problem. For example, a company could lose customers for a variety of reasons. Before dragging the customer service representatives to communication training and altering their scripts to add more "thank you" and "we appreciate your business," the organization must gather more data. Is competition increasing? Are demographics changing? Is there encroaching technology? This search, in addition to monitoring customers' opinions, should help point the company in the right direction. If the issue does turn out to be customer service, then where, specifically, is the problem? Customers could be waiting too long on hold, struggling with too many options to navigate, or finding themselves disconnected unexpectedly. Too many transfers to "another customer service representative" for an answer can drive a customer to impatience and turn business away. Perhaps the customer service representatives can't solve complex problems, give incorrect answers to questions, are impolite, or leave a "don't care" impression.[2]

Assessing Team Needs

When assessing the needs of your team, think of how it stacks up to others in the company. How does your team's performance rank compared to the others? Does it meet the average, or could it raise the bar on skills, setting a new standard for high performance? Would you like your team to be the "go-to" team for complex problem solving? How about being notorious for innovative ideas? For being the first group to apply a lean manufacturing tool and make it stick? If you have such a vision, then you are reading the right book to help you reach these goals. Begin thinking of the skills your team members need to apply to reach these critical goals and whether the expected outcomes are aligned to other stated and visible organizational needs.

For example, suppose your vision is to eliminate poor sampling techniques that result in high numbers of nonconformance for batches of drug product, resulting in delayed releases, extra quality testing, and potential scrutiny by regulatory agencies. Some of the issues are mislabeled samples, incorrect storage conditions, and samples that are kept in the wrong container or delivered to the lab after their expiration. In addition, the samples have a high frequency of contamination, which is proven to occur more often when technicians, rather than quality analysts, collect the samples.

Since on-time batch release is an organizational goal, solving the problem through an intervention would seem to be a good start. Let's say the team of technicians is a mixture of experienced samplers and those who are new to the role. You have watched the sampling process and observed that some of the experienced technicians take shortcuts, which they have passed on to the newer employees. These shortcuts, in combination with their low experience level, are likely causing most of the mistakes.

Here is one of many pathways you could take: Start by meeting with the staff and speaking about the department goal to eliminate sampling errors. Hand out sample bottles in the meeting and challenge all to practice taking off the cap and replacing it with one hand (make it a contest). Have other brief sessions to demonstrate correct storage conditions and the sterile technique for taking the sample (have your best sampler demonstrate). Remind all team members that following the procedure in full is the only acceptable way to handle sampling. Visibly and prominently monitor the success of each sample delivery on all the criteria you want to improve. You can also test the team members. Watch them put on sterile gloves in the correct manner, then swab for contaminants. Giving written and visual assessments, monitoring sampling success, and announcing team successes should bring about positive changes.

Assessing Individual Needs

When assessing the needs of individuals, the key is to not only analyze current behavior but to also look ahead. What is the person doing now that indicates a low level of skill? Does this employee avoid certain tasks that are clearly a part of the job, letting you or others do it instead? Would training the person to ace this task build strength in your team, lead to potential future advancement, help the business solve key losses, or save time in the existing process?

Let's take, for example, a person who continually asks other team members for help with tasks in an inventory database that the rest of the team has mastered. This person cannot locate lost inventory, prepare custom reports, or spot and correct missing entries. The team patiently helps the employee and gives pointers, but the fundamental problems remain, including slowness, errors, and taking the time of other team members. The impact on the team is severe when it is quarterly reporting time—at this crucial point, the entire group looks bad if there are inaccuracies. Extra time spent trying to help the less skilled team member builds resentment, and stress is also on the rise. When certain team members seem to get away with low performance, others on the team often blame the leader and may even slow down themselves.

What is the problem? Does the employee see it as a concern? The answer is that the problem is likely a combination of issues. The team is impacted by a weak link in the chain, so they will, with resentment, continue to support the weak employee so that they can meet team goals. The lesser skilled employee has seen no true personal impact for not mastering the system, and thus is in a comfort zone, with no incentive to struggle to gain the skills through purposeful practice. And so the person doesn't.[3]

Consider another example: A warehouse manager was frustrated with periodic inaccuracies in reported inventory levels. She got negative feedback from manufacturing that the components ordered from the warehouse were the incorrect amount, leading to sudden stops in production lines while more components were found and rushed over.

The manager thought about a specific inventory analyst (recently transferred from another department) who had been having problems turning in reports with incorrect inventory levels. When she asked the analyst to explain why he was struggling, he said he had difficulty recognizing inventory status levels, which the software expressed in different colors. Hesitantly, he explained he was color-blind and was trying to do the best he could. The need was identified as a slight customization of the system to clarify status using words in addition to color. So this situation was not a training need after all. The business need was legitimate, however, and the manager still got the credit for investigating and putting a solution in place.[4]

Taking Stock of Your Team

Use a simple method to look at more widespread problems with the entire team. Are there trends and weakness showing for the team? For example, is there only one expert on a critical task? Could the department use cross training to improve flexibility and response time? Pick a task and think of the skills of each team member in this task. Perhaps the job is to run knitting machines. The tasks may include changing out parts for different designs, troubleshooting poor quality product, and addressing minor stops.

A simple grid, with tasks across the top and team member names down the side, shows the skills for an entire department and is critical for planning purposes. Use a grid to measure the training progress for new hires, to identify experts and to plan further training sessions to build skills in weak areas.

The Risk of Having a Few Subject Matter Experts

Let's say your business occasionally suffers a big loss. It could be caused by a rare problem with the fire suppression system or a coolant system failure. When things go wrong in these systems, it is a very bad day, disrupting productivity, or causing scrapped product. Who in your organization is best at resolving these headaches quickly? Is it a thirty-five-year employee nearing retirement? Does the business hold its breath when this subject matter expert (SME) goes on vacation or is out with the flu?

Sometimes organizations get into this situation due to the subtle orchestrations of their SMEs. The experts want to jump in and save the company when needed. They will often be available on vacations. They may feel threatened when asked to train others, and therefore do poorly at this task. They may do a minimal job of drafting step-by-step procedures; after all, they don't want to share their "superpowers." We can't blame them, really. In return for their inability to develop competent successors, SMEs get job security and hero worship when they are able to pull the company back from the brink of disaster.

To solve this problem, start with a quiet heart-to-heart:

• Acknowledge the value of the SME. "Pat, you have a true superpower with the lyophilization unit. You helped us set up the unit and get it to freeze-dry our delicate product to a perfect dryness without damaging it. You are still our top go-to person on the unit whenever anything goes wrong." Now watch the look of pride expand across the face of your superhero.

- Next, explain your position. "Pat, I'm really nervous that you're our only expert on the system. It puts us in a shaky business situation, because you're our only hope to prevent loss in a serious breakdown. Also, we would love to use your expertise in designing a new system for our future expansion project. But since you are already tied to this one, we can't free you up until you develop a few additional experts to take your place. We want to turn you into a master trainer in the short term so we can free you up for this important work in the next few months. Who would you recommend we select for you to train?"

- Find a way to offer support and re-enforcement. "I hope you are excited about this opportunity. Please develop a list of objectives for the trainees, and let's meet weekly for a few minutes so they can tell me what they have learned. Let me know what I can do to help in those meetings. Thank you—I know this is going to work!"

If you do not have an expansion opportunity for the SME as in the example above, try to think of something else that will creatively meet the needs of this expert. Perhaps he or she is bored and would love to try something new. Since the world runs by incentives and rewards (as described in *Freakonomics* by S. Levitt and S. Dubner), you may need to get creative to help the SME find motivation and interest in teaching others. Consider, however, the alternative of a sudden loss of the intellectual capital that your organization depends on. You may have to do some coaching for reluctant SMEs if other motivational efforts fail.[5]

Develop More Superheroes

Employees are individuals, and their skills are different. Some are excellent at working with data: they move it around and chart it, and they analyze it's meaning. But if their role is to check and catalog inventory, then they are not really using those skills. Could you add something to their jobs that lets them use that strength? A conversation about their aspirations and strengths could turn up a skill you had not considered, and wouldn't you like to get that inventory analysis report off your back anyway? Just an idea, but one that allows you to delegate and to further develop their skills in data analysis.

Wouldn't it be nice to have a vibration analysis expert? Or a team of troubleshooters in the heat and friction arena? How about a waste expert to analyze the outgoing trash for low-cost recycling opportunities, reducing the organizations' overall spending on disposal and advancing the company toward environmental targets? Developing experts in these skills allows employees to grow and helps you solve certain business needs at the same time. We will cover more about development through delegation in Chapter 5.

As you can see, the offer of training and distinctive niche roles based on special skills can be a form of recognition, especially if you frame it right. In the discussion, be careful not to make it sound like you are piling on extra work. Make sure the employees know they are earning a special role, one that you have confidence they can fill, and that it is a good step for their development.

Identifying the Business Needs

You will find business needs communicated by top-level management, topics in town hall meetings, business unit objectives, or your own performance goals. If goals are not clearly communicated in your organization, encourage your direct leader to make business goals more transparent. Here is an example of a business problem and potential solutions. Let's say a business is struggling with excessive waste through quality defects; let's define the behaviors the employees will need to perform after training to meet the business need.

- Employees perform visual comparisons of questionable product to the quality standard
- Catalog defects and place them in reject bins with accuracy

In addition, they must define the skills and knowledge trainees will need to perform these behaviors. Can trainees remember to find the pictures of standard final product and do the

41

comparison? Are they recognizing defects? Can they fill out records with the correct information? Are they placing defects in the correct bin immediately after inspection so there is no possibility they will get moved back into the production line?   If the answer to any of these questions is no, then we have to ask further questions. Are they not doing the task correctly because of some barrier, such as the clarity and location of the quality standards? Is perhaps lighting a factor? Or is it a knowledge-based problem, such as recognition of defects and where to put them? The key is determining if it is a process problem, or a skills and knowledge problem. *Only the latter conclusion should send employees to a training intervention, designed to specifically meet that need.*

Gathering Data

One excellent way to determine whether there is a training need is to get pretty close to your team as they work in order to observe and document behavior. You can do this in an upfront and obvious way (picture yourself with a video camera and clipboard) or in less obtrusive ways, such as hanging around nearby, parking in a chair with your laptop, or drifting by to ask questions while keeping your eyes open.

I prefer a happy medium: asking questions of team members, probing for insight and gray areas in their understanding. Consider using these four excellent questions used by Toyota Production System experts when evaluating skills on the job:

- How do you do this task?
- How do you know you are doing it correctly?
- What do you do when you find a defect?
- How will you react to prevent further defects?[6]

As an employee answers these questions, look for confidence and full, detailed answers. These signs indicate that the person has a high level of expertise.

When you choose to simply observe, look for speed of execution and resolution, a short time frame for adjustments and changeovers, and a minimum of rejects, restarts, and help from other team members. The latter is an important metric, because getting help from another team member effectively doubles the time it takes to do a task. You might also observe and evaluate an employee's interactions with customers, coworkers, or other departments.

Another way to gather data is through the observations of others, such as co-workers, engineers, and other leaders in upstream and downstream departments. The quality control staff can help identify the behaviors that lead to missed defects. The maintenance department may be able to help you understand troubleshooting skills.

In addition, remember that the employees themselves are an excellent source of information. Ask your direct reports what skills they think they are missing that would help them to be better at their job. If the company has set a priority to save money, reduce defects, or prevent lost time, then explain this, and ask what they might need to meet those goals.

Five Whys: Diving Down through the Layers

A great amount of time and resources can be lost when people attend the wrong training for them. Companies often use training as a quick reaction to errors or significant losses. But if problems are not fully examined to find the root cause, training may be a big (and costly) miss.

Here's an example of an accident that happened in a production facility. On a Sunday morning, one of three technicians was climbing a ladder to reach the top of a 1,000-liter tank. He was holding on to the rail of the ladder with one hand and carrying a small container in the other. When he reached the top, he lifted a 25-pound stainless steel domed lid from the tank, propping it back on its hinge at a slight angle, where it usually stayed put. There was a small chain to secure the lid in that open position, but he did not use it. After the technician emptied the contents of the small container into the tank, he accidentally dropped the container, following it with his eyes as it bounced down the ladder to the floor. At that moment the tank lid slammed down on his hand, causing deep lacerations and broken bones.[7]

Let's explore this incident using a common root-cause process known as the "five whys" analysis. This is a simple way to dive deep into an issue to determine the foundational issues, by asking why after each proposed explanation for an incident.

1. Why did the lid drop onto the technician's hand? It is difficult to tell whether the tank lid is safely held back unless it is secured. In this case, the chain used to ensure the lid could not fall was unsecured.

2. Why didn't the technician use the chain to secure the lid? The technician claimed he had his hands full with a container and the handrail of the ladder. He could lift the lid, but did not have the dexterity to hold the ladder plus the container while also manipulating the chain into place.

3. Why did he not free a hand to take care of this important task? Other technicians carrying a small container can secure the chain. Because he was just adding a small amount of liquid and closing the lid again.

4. Why did the technician take this shortcut? Because even though he had been seriously injured before while working unsafely, and even though the department had safety training programs, there were no consequences (other than pain) to work safely every time.

5. Why were there no consequences for this employee who consistently worked unsafely? Because safe work practices were not a business priority. There were higher incentives for working quickly than for working safely, and there were no consequences for those who had taken unsafe shortcuts in the past.

So we can make a few conclusions in this case: safety training was not working to change unsafe behaviors, so more training was not the answer. A culture of accountability for safe working techniques needed to grow and be taken seriously.

Soon afterwards, leaders started very visible demonstrations of their concern for workplace safety. A vice president of the company entered work areas often to discuss safe work practices. Employees were given prizes for safety suggestions and were told to slow down to prevent accidents.

Get Agreement With Employees About Development Plans

Training can also be ineffective when we do not understand the individual's drive to succeed in learning. Some members of a team may be eager to encounter change because they want to gain new skills, and challenge themselves. Others, content to stay at the level where they have been for years, may have more negative feelings toward change. Some team members may feel defensive and threatened by the mere suggestion that they *need* training, and as a result have a negative attitude through the whole process. They are the first to say "The training was no good," which lets them distance themselves from their responsibility to put in the effort and learn. Negative attitudes about learning must be discovered, because without special feedback and coaching, these employees' training plan will crash and burn, adding to the mystery of why training often fails in organizations.

Let's take the example of a twenty-two-year veteran machine operator. She routinely takes longer than the standard amount of time to change over machinery, and she calls maintenance rather than attempting minor troubleshooting. An increase in her mechanical skills could improve productivity in her production line, and the tasks are clearly a part of her job. On-the-job instruction over the last two years has not made an appreciable difference, and the operator does not seem to see anything wrong with her performance. She may be resistant to change, since she is planning her retirement in four years. The case is made more complex by deeper problems that may be at work, such as unclear communication about productivity, a friendly mechanic who enjoys helping her, and a culture that accepts low performance. How is her leader to correct this problem?

The key is to talk. Leader and employee need to carve out time and discuss development. The leader should ask about concerns, bolster confidence, probe the employee's excuses, and explain business needs. Together they must discuss the future, challenge their thinking, and hammer out a plan that they both agree on. You can read more about this in Chapter 5, which discusses the performance management process.

Keep in mind a few typical perceptions that tend to hold people back from learning in the workplace. When people are allowed to do a partial job and rely on coworkers for the rest, a culture of low expectations begins that can be hard to correct in the long run. Another obstacle may be a perception that faster and more skilled operators get more responsibility and work with no increase in pay. If very few workers have been promoted, employees may not bother to try to stand out, seeing no future reward for themselves.

Also remember that when people are being asked to change, they want to know why. If they are not given specific and plausible reasons, they will imagine them instead. Change often triggers hostility and resistance, so it is no wonder that major change initiatives fail at high rates. To reduce resistance, be clear about the reasons and the expected outcome for the individual and the business.[8]

Also be clear that learning new skills is an important factor in future performance reviews. When this expectation is not formalized, employees have an easier time wriggling off the hook for gaining and using increased skills in the job. We will discuss how to succeed with this in Chapter 5.

The Needs of the Newly Hired

New employees are in a particularly interesting position. They want to prove themselves, look confident, and share their expertise. But often their team and leader are too busy for them. They may attend an orientation class, and then be left reading standard operating procedures with no one to show them around or answer their questions. After too much of this, their frustration levels will rise. The question often forms in the mind of a new hire: "Why should I stay here?"

49

In my experience, based on speaking with and surveying hundreds of new hires, the quality of onboarding—the process of integrating new employees into the company—is crucial. The more rocky the onboarding process, the sooner new hires will leave the company. You may have heard stories of people at your organization who left after a few days or months. This is a waste of time, money, and morale for your team. The amount of waste can actually be tremendous: all the time it takes to review resumes and interview candidates, the hours that new hires spend in orientation, the overextension of your current team, the work that goes undone, the errors of new hires as they learn their new role, the drop in morale of the team when they leave, and continued overwork by the team while the recruiting picks up again. Research puts this cost at approximately one and a half times the person's annual salary.[9]

Try to avoid a bad impression by putting together a welcoming onboarding process:

- Thank employees for choosing your company. Give them a little gift or note signed by team members.
- Provide an orientation class that ensures new hires know how to work safely: how to evacuate, how to get help, and how to avoid accidents in the work environment. Research shows accident rates are higher for new hires.[10]

- Tell new hires (in class or in person) how they can help the company. Discuss goals, targets, current priorities, and challenges so they know where to focus efforts from the very start.

These suggestions are offered as a minimum, so feel free to add more to your new hire program. You might ask subject matter experts to introduce their department functions, go over the product lines, use web technology to tap in with coworkers or close ties in other sites, meet the general manager for breakfast, lead a tour of the facility—anything that may help the new hires acclimate quickly and smoothly to the organization as a whole. Also, do not hesitate to introduce fun. As you will see in the next chapter, adults like engaging training classes.

Technical Training for New Hires

After the initial onboarding steps, another type of training is needed in order to get new hires working in their actual jobs. The success of this step depends on the degree of preparation that the department and organization make before new hires arrive. Let's go over three types of technical training for new hires.

Job Shadowing

Job shadowing, also called the buddy system, involves placing a new hire next to an experienced worker, who is asked to buddy up and show the new hire the ropes. An advantage of this approach is that it provides a one-to-one help from the trainer, and it is a hands-on approach

A disadvantage of this method is that if the expert gets pulled away, the trainee is expected to hold things together. Another potential weakness is inconsistency in training due to lack of structure and differing training skills. In fact, some experts may truly dislike training others.

Here is an example of the buddy system's drawbacks. Sally has worked at a manufacturing company for three months. She is assigned to work with Paul to learn how to use the carton packer and cruncher. It is a rather complex piece of equipment that can take a few days to learn and use successfully.

Paul is usually in a hurry and doesn't like to train new people. He feels he has the highest level of knowledge on the machine, and he isn't going anywhere, so why does he need to train anyone? Sally is slightly nervous about working with him.

On the first morning, Paul spends several minutes setting up the equipment while Sally stands to the side, watching him. He asks her to hold the crunch lever in the up position while he goes off to get the lubricant. He explains that sometimes the lubricant is needed, but not often. He quickly squirts some into a narrow gap in the gear system while the machine is still running. (The machine guard is not connected.) He then shows her how to take cartons off before they hit the floor.

Later, while Paul takes his break, he asks Sally to watch the machine. "Don't worry, it practically runs itself." Sally is anxious while he is gone. She hears a few noises that sound wrong and hovers near the emergency stop button, the only button that is clearly marked. She is late taking the crunched cartons off the belt, and several drop on the floor. She is relieved when Paul comes back. He continues to silently run the machine, occasionally making adjustments. He doesn't seem to be in the mood to talk and answers her many questions with one or two words.

Notice the lack of a manual, labels, and a communicative trainer.[11] Trainees in these situations have more anxiety, are more likely to hurt themselves and tend to learn by making mistakes.

Structured On-the-Job Training (S-OJT)

Basically, S-OJT means adding structure around the training approach. Instead of a buddy, manufacturing leaders select a trained trainer. Instead of taking an off-the-cuff approach, the trainer teaches from an approved manual or standard procedure. Before signing off, the trainer evaluates the trainee's skills with a quiz or other method.

A potential weakness of this method is that supervisors often see two workers rather than a trainer and a trainee. They may continue to urge high productivity numbers from two people who are busy with learning and teaching. Another drawback is that even in an S-OJT environment, it is still easy for new hires to make mistakes and hurt themselves.

Simulation Training

Simulation areas are set up in a dedicated area, use dedicated equipment, and are highly structured. The end-to-end teaching of the topic is self-driven by the trainee, with minimal direction but several structured evaluations by experts. This type of training is used mainly in the military, the medical field, in training pilots, and some industrial settings. Designing simulation training is time intensive up front. But once the design is done, simulation-training facilities need minimal care.

A research study on technical training compared self-led simulation training with the same topic taught by an instructor. Both methods resulted in a significant increase in knowledge and skills as measured by pretests and posttests. But participants in the simulation group retained more of the information, as measured three months after training. They also rated their own confidence on the topic more highly than the other group did, and their confidence levels positively correlated with performance ratings.[12]

Those results favor simulation training, but not all organizations have the internal expertise to build a simulation training area or the money to have a vendor set one up for them. You can spend loads of money on 3D simulation software that shows trainees the inner workings of the equipment through virtual means. However, you can also start easier by simulating entry-level technical training, exposing trainees to low-stakes repetitive techniques that help build expertise.

At a pharmaceutical company, I designed a simulation area to teach eighteen general technical topics to sixty new bio-technicians. Previously, all training was done at a one-to-one ratio. With the simulation method, one trainer facilitated the learning of five to eight trainees, all rotating through each learning station. The typical training time was reduced by two-thirds, and the trainees' competence levels were highly rated by leaders. The new hires were able to leave the simulation area and get straight to work, reducing the typical burden on the trainers and supervisors.

Keep in mind that some jobs take a few years to learn completely, especially when it comes to judgment, advanced troubleshooting, and complex and expensive equipment and batch setups, For those types of tasks, simulation training is likely unreachable, and your organization will have to rely on S-OJT instead. For simpler topics, or for tasks that require the development of dexterity, a simulation training area is the ultimate in cool and effective training methods.[13]

The Need for Basic Skills

Some people in technical or manufacturing jobs have minimal basic skills in math and reading. Perhaps they quit school to get a low-paying job. They may be relying on experience to eventually get them into higher paying technical positions.

This strategy may work for a while. But as the pressures and needs of businesses change, people who were not expected to read technical materials and perform calculations in the past may begin to struggle. Leaders may need long-term employees to increase their basic skills in order to use increasingly complex software or to read and follow lengthy and complex procedures. In these situations, low-skilled workers are at a disadvantage, under pressure, and probably demoralized. So how should leaders proceed?

Unfortunately, there is no silver bullet for this one. The training gaps here tend to be fundamental. They go back to the quality of education people were offered and the effort they put into achieving these skills.

One long-term idea is to require that all job candidates submit to standardized testing to prove they have the basic skills for the job. These tests must be valid for the specific job that candidates wish to enter. For example, a math test for a mechanic candidate cannot be more complex than the type of math the job requires. For more information on employment testing, see the EEOC's Uniform Guidelines for Employee Selection.[14]

Pre-employment testing requires a lot of work to set up, but it offers a huge advantage. It allows employers to test prospective employees in a way that predicts their future success in the job. Then employers no longer need to ask "Will they have the basic skills to get through the training period successfully?" and "What should we do with them if they don't?"

Case Study: PGT Industries

Let's look at how basic cognitive testing (ACT's WorkKeys assessments) made huge changes for PGT Industries, the United States' leading manufacturer and supplier of residential impact-resistant windows and doors. In 2006, the company partnered with a local community college (Rowan-Cabarrus Community College in Salisbury, NC) to analyze the common skills needed to successfully work in the company. The positions most often required skills in math, reading, observation, and locating information. Once the analysis, also known as job profiling, was complete, the employer knew what level candidates needed to score to succeed in their new job. The company then had candidates take the tests. The tests were designed and administered by ACT, the organization that also does College Entrance Testing. The following business impacts were noted:

- Performance-related turnover for new hires dropped by 30 percent in the first ten months.
- The hiring process became more streamlined and recruiting costs went down. PGT now has a database of hundreds of prequalified applicants with documented skill levels.
- Training costs were reduced by 50 percent, due to a greatly diminished need to provide basic skills training before job skills training.

The amount of time for performance to reach full competence level was reduced from six months to three months.

Case Study: 911 Communication Center, Lexington County, SC

Facing high turnover (the average job stay was two years, partly due to the complexity of computer and communication systems), along with a six- to twelve-month average training period, this county's public safety office was spending too much per new hire. With WorkKeys testing, they had the confidence that new hires had the skills to succeed with the job requirements. After the implementation, no employee was discharged for skills issues, and the overall turnover changed from 30 percent to 15 percent, a big difference for the agency.[15]

Can Training Be Free?

Beware of "free training" from vendors. In one instance, a group of maintenance workers were invited to a talk about bearings. They were promised an in-depth seminar on best practices regarding bearings maintenance and replacement. What they got instead was a sales pitch by a vendor trying to get a foothold in their business. The trainees got free ball caps, but learned nothing they could apply to make improvements in their jobs. They complained to the decision makers who allowed the vendor in, and those leaders learned their lesson about the value of free training. Training time should be selectively applied. If it is not aligned with a business need, and there is no plan to show it to be effective, then it contributes to the perception that training is a waste of time.[16]

Wrapping Up

It might seem like a daunting task to keep all the factors in mind in order to pinpoint the correct need before going forward with a training class. But it is important to reduce the waste that typically comes with the field of training. Only "reality-based training"—training that is both aligned to business priorities and based on the reality of observable or measurable needs—should be the focus.[17] You should be starting to get a picture of how important every step is to prevent the waste that contributes to unsuccessful training in so many organizations. There is of course the unfortunate and often maligned "Required Training" which is most of the time conducted due to regulations. But even this can be a worthwhile effort with excellent design and plans to transfer that knowledge into better compliance behaviors. We will look into this in the next chapter, and incidentally, we will attempt to banish forever, that scourge of classrooms: Death by PowerPoint.

Before moving on to the next chapter, take a few minutes to write down some of your business headaches that you think are related to training: the behaviors, skills, and knowledge that are missing. Go to www.BuildingGiants.com to download the training plan form in the "book-building giants/training plan" tab, and make some notes in the first section.

Chapter 3: Training-Designed for Success

A Standard Approach to Effective Training

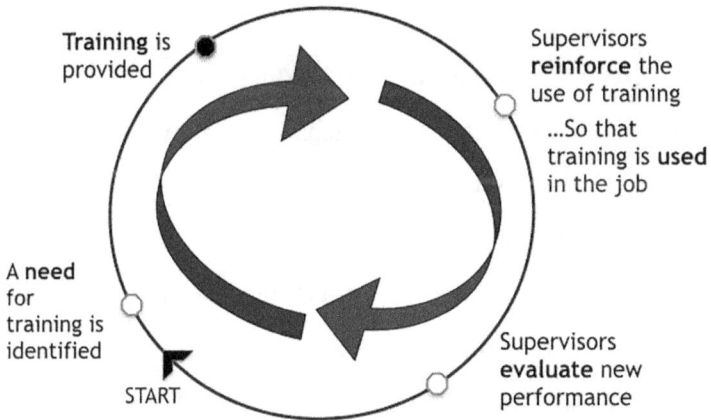

Training is provided

Supervisors **reinforce** the use of training

...So that training is **used** in the job

A **need** for training is identified

START

Supervisors **evaluate** new performance

Introduction

Outstanding books are filled with complete and explicit instructions for how to deliver training classes that engage, even entertain participants, receiving rave reviews on smile sheets, and earning genuine applause at the end of a class. But since this book acknowledges that the training class is just one part of several critical elements, we will focus instead on using a training session as a bridge, enabling learners to make use of new, needed skills in the job. If training is engaging, enriching (even hilarious at times) we are on our way to the possibility of successful transfer of skills to the workplace. First let's look at what not to do, so you can draw a clear comparison between effective and waste of time-styles of training.

This Chapter Will Help You:

- Recognize ineffective training techniques
- Determine in advance how to measure effectiveness of your next learning intervention
- Draft SMART learning objectives
- Evaluate students in their accomplishment of class objectives
- Plan effective training

A quick note: If you are not the one who will put together training classes, then just read enough of this chapter to recognize ineffective training and how to avoid it. Then go on to Chapter 4 and learn about how to make sure your organization sees the most benefit from the training effort.

The Fire Hose Pours Out Training

Let's say it is important that employees know how to act when auditors come up to talk with them during an inspection for compliance. To get good audit results (the business need), employees are expected to know and describe the quality systems, protocols and procedures they work within (this is the behavior they need to show to auditors). The specific skill they need to learn and master is to reply to questions pleasantly and accurately, using few words. A typical solution would be for a company to pull people off the floor and show some PowerPoint slides of likely questions and ideal answers and then return the employee to the job

The job of an auditor is to examine organizational systems to be sure they meet compliance objectives. One way they delve deeply into those systems is to quiz employees. They walk up to employees while they are working and ask them something about a procedure, or something they observe, or even an opinion about a task, and then they fall silent, often boring their eyes into those of their victim. They are watching and listening closely. They wait an extra long beat after the person stops speaking, hoping they will fill the silence with more information out of nervousness. Often employees keep talking, as the auditor gives the impression they are not satisfied with what they have heard. This is when auditors find the juicy stuff: Exceptions, excuses, errors and general slip ups as their target rambles on. They may fold their arms, raise an eyebrow and ask probing questions as the person trails off. Behind the auditor, the company leaders wring their hands, clear their throats and add to the general tension and collective perspiration.

Now let's take a look at the results of the training. When the auditors come, leaders of the employees are hoping to observe short, accurate and pleasant responses to auditors. Alas... nine operators talk too much, without directly answering the question, potentially alerting auditors to other issues to look into. Five operators talk too little, not answering direct questions, causing auditors to ask more and more questions, and to look even less convinced they are getting the information they require. Five to six of the most experienced operators do pretty well, with short, accurate and confident answers.

Let's examine the impact of the training effort.[1] Table 3.1 summarizes the effectiveness of the Auditor Prep Training efforts, using four levels of training effectiveness, which we outlined in Chapter 1.

Effectiveness of Auditor Prep Training		
Level 1	Did the learners like the training?	We do not know, we didn't do smile sheets
Level 2	Did the student learn the training content?	We do not know, we didn't test or observe them in class
Level 3	Did the students use what we taught them?	No, a number of operators talked too much or too little
Level 4	Did this training help the business?	No, the auditors had a poor opinion of learners' cooperation, and uncovered more problems

The fire hose approach to training means that we are "telling" people what to do, but not teaching them how to do it. Adult learners need some time and opportunity to apply new concepts, with activities, practice and reflection to deepen understanding, leading to the ability to perform the tasks when called upon. As we go through the key points in this chapter, you should pick up on some interesting truths about adult learners.

In the case of "Auditor Prep Training," someone very experienced, such as the Director of Regulatory Affairs, could have taken on the role of instructor, and after demonstrating, could have had people partner up, and held contests both for best intimidating auditor and best answers under pressure. This would have more fully prepared potential "targets" with a realistic simulation of skills before the start of the inspection. Back on the job, leaders could have been given the assignment to ask two additional high-pressure style questions and coach their team members with additional feedback. This deepens the experience in the real context of the job.

Planning in Advance for Effectiveness

It is helpful to decide in advance to what level you would evaluate your next training effort. A good general rule is to evaluate at higher levels when the training is critical to the business, and the project is rather visible. If you are expected to report the outcomes of your training and you need "rock-star" status to prove your value as a leader or training professional, then save time for evaluation, even if higher management is not asking for it. Also if you have a specific goal to change a part of the business, and you determine it can be done through training, then it is a good idea to go further in your evaluation effort so that you have concrete evidence when it comes to the end of the year performance review or the conclusion of the project.

If you plan to go all the way to level 4 or even to level5, return on investment, it is important that you do the analysis and have some starting data. You can get this from the needs assessment. Can you answer the question: how many losses are happening at what frequency? If it is defects, how many pieces are lost? Is it scrap material? How much by weight? Is it communication breakdowns leading to losses? If it is lost customers, employee complaints, injuries, or machine down time, then what is the frequency? Each of these metrics could be a serious concern to an organization. To be a rock star, first use the tips from the last chapter to confirm the problem stems from a lack of skills or knowledge, then let's set the stage to show how you will remove the problem, and deliver measurable and credible improvements when the training process is finished.

For example, if you are placed in charge of assuring a better audit this year, and in the past, a weak element was the responses from operators on the floor, then give some time to prepare students adequately, with practice and evaluation.

Planning for Success by Being Explicit

You may have heard about the acronym SMART at company goal setting classes. The acronym is slightly different for different companies.

S – Specific

M –Measurable

A – Attainable or actionable or agreed

R – Related or relevant or realistic

T – Time based or timely

Using all the elements included in SMART forces you to think through the problem and communicate it clearly to others. When you finish with your needs analysis from Chapter 2, finish at the point where you have an excellent guess as to what behaviors students need to apply in the job to bring about the expected change. Now when you are pulling together the actual learning session, express what is to be learned to meet that business need in a statement with five elements of SMART.

For example, if customer complaints reveal the problem of grit in the instant mushroom soup, we will need to focus in on more effectively removing contaminants from ingredients prior to the compounding step. Analysis of the task in the job reveals that a visual inspection of the mushrooms after the wash step is the right point to identify contaminated ingredients, which is then to be diverted for an additional wash cycle. A "SMART" objectives for training will then be: *"Perform a 15 second inspection of ingredients visually for contaminants using lighted lenses and determine if additional wash cycles are needed."*

Going back to an earlier example of the high number of "lost pallets" resulting in late customer shipment and fines, our analysis shows that forklift drivers are not navigating the inventory system fully to troubleshoot the misplaced pallets, including accessing archived files, tracing code input discrepancies and identifying other handlers of the product in question. In this case, one SMART objective for students could be: *"Quickly and confidently navigate to all tracking system pages, and name the function of each page."* Another could be: *"Investigate code input discrepancies, discovering the specific employee involved in the movement of a particular pallet."* Can you see how, when these types of statements are made, the student has fair warning of how they are to succeed in training? Also, the instructor now has a skill level to shoot for and evidence to gather to prove they have successfully taught the students.

Next, the teaching method must support the action needed. If 30 compounders need to be taught how to effectively conduct a visual inspection, including taking random samples and using lighted magnifying lenses, then naturally we have to think about how to make this feasible and effective. (Hint, the fire hose method makes the least amount of sense, as this type of training calls for some practice and confirmation of skill.)

Tricky Ways to Test Learners Without Being Obvious

A little secret: the fire hose approach is not fun for instructors _or_ participants. First, let's lower the pressure on the fire hose. With a little imagination, you do not have to present a 40-slide deck with densely packed text and a long test at the end. You can replace much of that content and approach. To involve and engage students, keep the lectures to small bites and add exercises to show, involve, explain, etc. Can you take a quick video? Or are there already dozens of great videos on your topic on the Internet? Can you pass around examples of defects? How about taking students out of the classroom altogether to show them specific tasks in the workplace then returning to a quiet place to discuss what was seen and performed?

Going back to our recent example, have students examine and evaluate mushroom samples under the same kind of scope that is to be used in the job and divert the contaminated components. This hands-on practice is much better than speaking about defects, or showing them pictures of defects in slides. Throw in some samples of dirty mushrooms with clean ones and be sure they can pick out the bad stuff.

For the slides leftover —scrutinize them. Reduce each busy slide to key concepts and use the extra time to add in creative techniques. Reduce the words and substitute fascinating pictures. Ask thought-provoking questions that start discussions (likely your audience already knows at least some of your topic). Removing multiple bullets and lines in small font and replacing them with action may actually be easy in some situations. For example, in a measurement class, instead of showing example after example of correctly rounding off calculations, ask a volunteer in the class to round them off, and the rest to check her work. Instead of telling them what defects are in pictures, let students spot them on actual examples.

The ideas listed near the end of this chapter are especially helpful for several reasons: They reduce the boredom of too many slides, they keep the brain and sometimes the body moving, and they allow application or practice of the concepts they must learn, easing the transition from short-term to long-term memory.

Research shows that the attention span of humans lasts only 20 minutes or so on average before people drift off and (in their heads) write groceries lists, make vacation plans and finish arguments with their spouses.[2] Breathing slows, eyes go unfocused and the lecture becomes background noise as students sink into lethargy. You may have even heard a few snores as an instructor or fellow student.

In this situation, students commonly drift off during straight lecture-style training sessions that last over 20-30 minutes. They perk up again near the end. See this in figure 3.1.

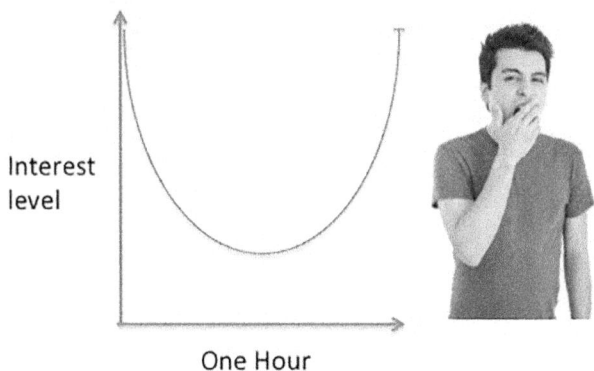

One Hour

This means to keep students with you, you will need to change the teaching method often. Show a few slides then show a video, a few more slides, and then it is time for a contest. A bit later, let's all get up and do some flip charts. Now how about a demonstration? Your goal is not to switch tactics so often that students are confused, rather to use a few, simple activities to reinforce the learning while keeping the listlessness away.

When you vary the teaching method by introducing an activity or some other action oriented approach every 20 minutes or so, the change keeps interest levels high, and students do not have a chance to droop. See this in Figure 3.2.

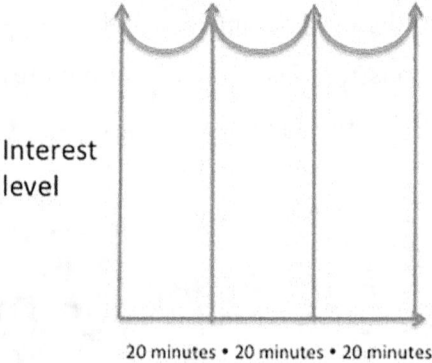

Interest level

20 minutes • 20 minutes • 20 minutes

A Little Bit About Adult Learning Theory

If you think adults do not like games, toys, skits, puzzles or videos etc. in favor of sitting still and working to pay attention through slideshows, then you yourself may not have been exposed to well-planned, interactive and effective training. Your model may be school, where lectures and homework with demonstrations, exercises and hands-on practice were more rare the farther in school you went. (Of course there were exceptions...you must have a memory of dancing with an assigned partner and those chemistry and biology labs.) But your more recent memory may be lecture format, where you hoped to retain enough to get you through the exam.

By contrast, there is nothing quite like a room full of mature adults working together to analyze their own personality styles and then form teams to build an egg capsule to drop over a balcony, team by team. When a team unwraps their unbroken egg, the cheers raise the roof and the debrief reveals how each personality style was necessary to accomplish that feat. It really is supposed to be all about the learner, but in these kinds of scenarios, the instructor is having fun too. The interest level significantly drops when trainers read lots of text off slides.[3]

Getting the Class to Participate With Active Learning

Engaging a class full of adults might seem like a daunting task but making the classroom an active place helps students use skills in the job. Active learning techniques are more effective than the long-standing tradition of simply listening to lectures, perhaps taking notes, and occasionally asking a question or two. Once training classes turn away from the traditional (boring) approach, and students are involved in the learning process actively, smile sheet ratings go way up, and positive word of mouth spreads. There might even be a "standing room only" situation.

Creative Training Techniques

The following are simply a list of ideas to convert boring lectures to blood pumping, engaged participation. Jot down your favorites, and come back to this list when you are planning a new training program.

- Ask open-ended questions to spark discussion. If someone asks you a question, see if the class can answer it for you. This helps you to act more as a facilitator than a lecturer, leaving the class to engage more actively.

- Ask students to doodle a picture that relates to the class and hang them up at break time for a relevant laugh. Or go with pipe cleaners, marshmallow people or silly putty animals. Ask students to evaluate and award fabulous prizes for best efforts. Doodling while listening has been shown to enhance learning, and retention of knowledge by 29%[4].

- Flip charts! Ask the students to come up with ideas, examples, diagrams, questions, concepts or explanations. Use themes, silly or otherwise to get creative juices flowing. Give them the nice smelling markers and assign groups to design a group tee shirt complete with logo.

- Do a team building exercise that involves prizes and fun. You could develop a trivia contest about the organization for a fun learning exercise. Get teams playing "Get to know you BINGO" as an icebreaker. Check the Appendix for rules for a few simple games and resources.

- Invite teams to be creative and give them an exercise to think outside the box (try an inkblot test from the internet, or a contest to build a useful gadget from paperclips.)

- Ask participants to put together a skit or short presentation. Use a smart phone to record it (make sure you ask permission if you decide to put a video on YouTube, you do not want to "out" someone in the witness protection program, for example.)

- Ask participants to use smart phones to search for answers to obscure but vital questions in the form of a contest with "fabulous prizes."

- Create a life-sized board game (use tape or posters on the floor), with students having to answer questions to advance.

- Create a discussion panel of "visiting experts" and have the class as the audience, asking questions.

- Do a demonstration- Freely using participants. For example, I used colored plastic balls to represent protein molecules and had students act as chemical bonds by grabbing the right colored balls and letting them go at the correct time to demonstrate the steps of protein purification. When students are pretending to be a chemical bond while rolling brightly colored balls that get loose (or stolen by another participant or the instructor), the lessons are rather memorable. Feedback came back to your author over the next six years of how well learners remembered and enjoyed that particular demonstration.

- Do group projects: Have learners investigate a claim, find a disconnect in the process flow, work out a measurement and math problem, reorganize data to discover patterns, perform a root cause analysis on a real incident, map a process in order to discover waste, or research and teach the rest of the class a key concept.

- Don't forget a debrief period! Any group exercise that involves a chance of analysis, discovery or team building deserves a careful debrief with students to discuss their insights and reiterate the main point of the exercise.

Many more examples exist; you can get them from books or make them up on your own on the spot. There is nothing like a flip chart, a group and colorful markers to get the blood moving. At least one class participant puts a marker dot on their nose, trying to catch the scent of lime, orange or cherry. (It is kind of cruel to put out the regular, chemical-smelling markers isn't it?)

A note about your learners: It is extremely rare that they fold their arms and refuse to participate in a class activity, including brainstorming, case studies, and egg dropping, even role-play (although this should be used sparingly, by volunteers, and only if you really need it, as some people are petrified about speaking in front of even small groups). Be sensitive to excessive complexity and silliness. Activities should be there to re-enforce the learning concepts. So wearing a grass skirt and playing luau music might mystify your learners if they are there to learn about concepts in contamination control. Also, if it takes several minutes plus repetition to explain the activity you want students to do, it may be too complex and lengthy to really work. Remember, if there is no point, adult learners will realize there is nothing in it for them, and fun or not, they will likely decide it was a waste of their time. So make it relevant.

What about policy-based training, where learners need to read the exact words of instructions and regulations? You may be asking, "How am I supposed to teach an active and engaging class if I am expected go over the materials with them word for word?" I am glad you asked, as there are solutions for these situations. Let's say the requirement is that learners know a procedure exactly as written, and sign off to that effect on a record. You can still have participants, in groups, analyze a passage, demonstrate it, critique it, report it, read them in shifts, have contests for listing the steps in order, etc. Give fabulous prizes, have them draw pictures, have "Jeopardy!" contests or have them analyze videos. Make sure students read the applicable sections of text, not on slides, but from handouts, mixed with related activities to help it sink in.

Back to SMART and Confirmation of Learning

Now that you have had a fun break working on creative thoughts and classroom activities, let's get back to evaluating the student's learning. Surprise! We have done much of the work already! For example, if you have a SMART objective for students to perform a root cause analysis of a recent real incident, you can evaluate their efforts as they do this task in small groups. If another skill was to perform an investigation to identify those who handled a particular pallet of inventory, then give students a pallet ID number, and access to the system to discover those who worked with that pallet. In other words, the class activities are a reflection of what the students will need to do in the job. Obviously introduce the concepts first through a few slides, lectures, explicit written instructions, or simply vocal direction, either in a class or at the job site itself.

The method chosen should be close to real conditions if possible. For example, with the Heat Treatment Department probe handling training, (see Ch. 1) training was conducted with a flip chart, pen, and a broken probe. A small group for each shift met with the leader at the furnace itself, quite a cheap solution for the return on investment they realized.

Here are some more examples of great exercises. Not only do they tend to replace boring slides, but they tell you if your class is meeting their course objectives.

If the SMART Objective is:	Then try this as a subtle test:
Find lost inventory in 12 minutes or less.	Have groups of four locate lost inventory in the tracking system in under 12 minutes.
Write comprehensive Standard Operating Procedures (SOPs)	Have groups write SOPs for changing a tire or using the coffee maker and have others evaluate them.
Recognize defects and correctly disposition them.	Give learners defects to analyze and categorize, filling out (fake) records

Notice that the SMART objectives start with a verb, and are intended to perform three key actions:

1. Objectives give students clear expectations so they will know what success looks like for them.

2. Objectives align with the behaviors needed in the job to alleviate the business problem

3. Objectives are also a list of skills for instructors to use for evaluating students. This helps a trainer to decide if new skills and knowledge were learned, and to differentiate the performance of individuals.

Try and avoid setting an objective for students to "understand... or gain knowledge of..." because it is difficult to evaluate the knowledge and understanding the students have picked up, without giving them a paper and pencil test at the end of class. A long, detailed exam is not really fair after a low energy, wordy slide presentation. Instead, look for signs the students can translate learning into action. Can they give feedback using a framework? Can they discover a root cause? Can they reduce an escalating conflict? Can they troubleshoot a fault? Can they pick out defects? When you find the answers to these types of questions, then you have evidence of performance that has been raised through training.

Going back to our example of the new inventory tracking system, if training is not hands on, occurring in the system itself, or a mock up system often called a "sandbox," then this is almost sure to cause poor transference of skills to the job. Imagine a student repeating the concepts in their head over and over again in order to keep the details in their short-term memory, while they rush from the classroom to the desk and repeat the key learning in the real system. It can't work, especially if the training ended on a Friday afternoon. After a weekend of mowing the lawn, changing diapers and watching movies, the student will have little recall, and may even have difficulty following explicit written instructions. Plentiful practice and evaluation should also occur in the system, with students performing the types of tasks they will need to do on the job confidently and quickly. A paper and pencil test makes less sense in this scenario.

If the training is more conceptual, then a written test may make sense for the session, and a pre and post format is excellent for this. (See an example in the Appendix.) This method takes the pressure off students by giving them a chance to guess at the quiz before class, therefore warning them as to what answers they will need to know by the end of class. If the tests are collected after the first attempt and again after the second, instructors can get a measure of what the students learned during the class. Knowing the questions ahead of time also causes students to pay closer attention to key concepts during lectures, knowing they need to have the right answer on that topic later.

Strategies for Skill Transfer to the Job

During the class design phase it is time to start thinking through strategies for transferring the new skills to the job.

1. Training Class ....
2. then a miracle occurs
3. Results

"I think you should be more explicit here in step two"

Do you remember this cartoon? It is a good time to put in place some ideas to help students to use their new skills in the real context: their work area. Can the instructor assign work tasks to students to perform in the job? With the agreement of their leadership, they certainly can. An example could be an assignment to perform a task in the new way and then report the outcome, for example, in communication classes, ask students to report back the differences they see in making presentations, using skills in difficult discussions, or changing the tone from negative to positive in customer emails. Those who report back get an internal certification, or a fabulous prize. Here are a few other examples:

- Assign students to perform 5 why root cause analyses for the next 3 problems they see, and offer a prize.
- After a coaching class, assign the leaders to coach at least 2 employees and write up a summary, stating what went well, and what they would change next time. (Have them leave the employees unnamed for privacy.)
- After Train the Trainer class, have students perform training for others and have their students fill out smile sheets for them. They are turned in for an internal certification.
- After Project Management class, have students check in with the project status and also write up a post mortem about what went well and what they would change next time.

Though these are great ideas, they are likely at least somewhat out of the instructor's control if they do not directly manage the students. This key weakness and solutions will be fully explored in the next chapter.

Dragging Students to Class

What about mandatory training? When you, either as a leader or an instructor, are faced with a classroom of cranky students about to be taught yet another system for handling inventory, or tracking expense or logging job safety analyses, you may ask yourself, "How can I succeed here?" It boils down to this: the students aren't likely "with you" from the start, a serious obstacle to learning. You may have partial success but research shows that purposeful change management strategies improve the success of projects involving a change in behavior, and this starts earlier than the arrival to the classroom by largely unwilling participants.

Change management strategies involves helping students to see why this change is necessary: why is it good for them, why is it good for the business, and why they will ultimately be able to succeed on the other side of this change. People often react very negatively to change, becoming hostile, confused and often angry. When you answer the question "why?" and people understand it, it helps that negativity to go away, and that is a start in getting people to accept the change and desire to learn the concepts[5].

If, as a leader or training professional, you realize your students are not on board with a training class that they perceive involves a painful and unwanted change, it is a better investment in time to stop and go over the "why's", emphasizing the improvements this change will make on the business, for the people involved, in the job going forward. In other words advertise and market very positively what the new systems will do to make life easier.

Empathize with your class if they were not told why the change needed to take place. Then explain why the changes are necessary for the business, why now, and why they will help (and be creative here). For example: "This new system is going to virtually illuminate reconciliation errors, making your life so much easier and less frustrating. It is so slick it will even point you in the direction of the likely cause of errors. Let me show you why this system is the best thing since sliced bread. I'm proud that our company has found and can afford such a great system to move us all to the next level."

You could also ask them to write the reasons why they do not want to be there on sticky notes and put them on a wall then walk around and put them into categories. Some comments might be about a fear a failure. Others are too busy, some think it is not worth it, or too frustrating. Thank participants for identifying some of the typical pains encountered during transitions. Reassure them that they can learn it and you are there to help them. Let them know the company is setting time aside so they can master the new skills (if inadequate time is put aside make sure to inform the people who are sponsoring the project and emphasize that time spent in learning is better than time spent in undoing errors).

The better, longer-term solution for the next project or the next wave of people is to get involved early with the target audience. Start speaking positively about the project early in the plan, explaining why the change is needed, what it will do for the organization, and what positive impacts can be expected. Share the transition plan early and collect feedback about the change. People want to be part of the planning for changes that affect their work, so engage them early when possible.

Much of the frustration caused in workplace change is the sense that people are not in control. Allowing information flow and a chance to give feedback reduces the anxiety and builds the desire to change behavior and to engage in learning.[5]

What is a Fabulous Prize, Anyway?

This is generally something light-hearted and fun, often used to create a spirit of competition and urgency in attaining training goals. Try to find good prizes on a budget that manage to increase the visibility and brand of the organization's training efforts. Goofy, stylish or otherwise visible pens or pencils with a learning quote on it are usually economical. Squeeze balls, tiny trophies, or stuffed animals work as well. As a student in a 3 day long (somewhat excruciating) class on the Code of Federal Regulations for Good Manufacturing Practices, I was part of a group who competed with others to scramble through the regulations to find the answers for certain compliance scenarios. The instructor mysteriously promised that the winning group would receive an "attaché case." Sure enough, as part of the winning group, my teammates and I were awarded a 2x3 inch leather attaché case, meant to carry and present business cards. Clever!

Wrapping up

Having an engaging classroom experience with SMART objectives, and with instructors conducting active teaching with evaluations is a great start. Instructors use smile sheets to gather feedback to continuously improve so they can fine-tune their style and understand what students felt about the instruction, learning activities and other elements of the class. Even if sessions are taught in the work environment, in intermittent, short segment classes, or by online means, feedback is a gift to instructors for their improvement.

The mistake employers often make is to stop there, or at best to apply a paper and pencil test and call it a day. Research shows that although positive reactions to training as captured on smile sheets (level 1) are positively associated with measured learning during the class (level 2) there is no significant positive correlation with the training behaviors being used in the job (level 3). We have to go further to ensure success with training projects.[6] Read on to see how to make sure students change behavior as a result of training. This is the most critical as well as the most overlooked part in the training cycle. AND, this is your chance to see performance zoom and see real results.

For your assignment: On your worksheet, please add SMART objectives for your training intervention plan, as well as active learning and evaluation methods. Now is the time to capture the creative training techniques that have struck you as a perfect alternative to endless slides.

Chapter 4: Changing Behavior After Training

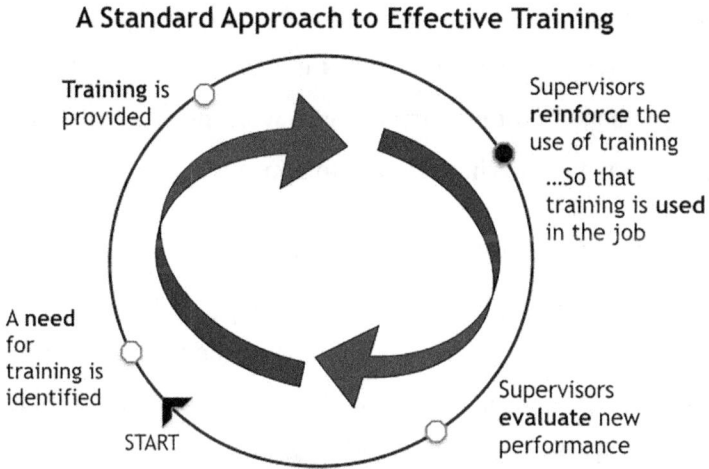

A Standard Approach to Effective Training

Training is provided

Supervisors reinforce the use of training

...So that training is used in the job

A need for training is identified

START

Supervisors evaluate new performance

A Story of Waste

Picture this, three employees from a team of 10 have returned from a one-day class on Lean Manufacturing. The class was enlightening, with fun exercises mixed with lecture to explore lean tools, especially process mapping and waste reduction. Since they have been out a day, the rest of the team has been severely stretched, and productivity is way down. The team has to work longer hours the rest of the week to make the required units. The following week, one of the learners, Don, shows a work assignment from the class to his supervisor, Jayne. It is the first she has heard that there would be an assignment, and she looks it over, realizing she is expected to let this employee and the other two learners tackle an improvement project to reduce waste in the production line. Up to her eyebrows in emails and past due crises, she nods and says, "Go ahead and find something to work on," and then she turns back to her list of purchase orders to approve.

Don tries to round up the other two to discuss their class assignment, with the thought that they could do it together. But the class is already in the past for them, and they are still in catch up mode from the chaos of last week. They ask to put it off until the next week. So Don lays the assignment down on his desk with tests results, batch records and quality alerts. When he saw it again a week later, he sighed, and laid it in a drawer. No one had mentioned the assignment since the class, and he was busy after all.

The memories, which had a chance to become long term, are quickly fading away, even though the class was interactive and full of great content. The skills and knowledge have not deepened, the insight and reflection that comes with practice did not happen, and the class soon becomes a vague memory of the course's key message: That organizations often generate quite a lot of waste.[1,2]

Training has not succeeded
until behavior has changed...

Introduction-and Congratulations

Congratulations! You have arrived at one of the most crucial points in performance, the point at which you can make a terrific impact on the success of a training effort. Now the focus is on not letting all that learning get lost in the daily grind and distractions outside of the classroom. The secret is to imagining the students are still in the classroom, even though they have returned to the job.

This Chapter Will Help You:

- Plan efforts to transition students to use new skills and knowledge to realize needed business results.

- Support the use of learned concepts after the training to create long-term memory of the new skills and knowledge.

Skills Erosion: Up to 90% Without Intervention

Experts agree that training retention is notoriously dismal in much of organizational training, and that, for the typical adult, recalling more than 10%-20% of the content within a few weeks of the training is all that can be expected.[3] Certainly the instructional design and the ability to apply the learning are tremendous factors in the potential success of a training program. Let's start with a quick explanation of how humans learn.

People build knowledge in predictable ways, through the movement and processing of information in the brain. The introduction of information is processed briefly by the senses, then it moves on to short-term memory (STM), where it remains for only a small amount of time. To keep information in the STM, it needs to be repeated, or else it will be lost. Now the trick is to support retention, by moving the information over to the long-term memory.

Repetition is still a factor here, and the pairing of information in the STM (also called the working memory) with similar information retrieved from long-term memory (previously learned information) is also critical.[4] Picture a person learning to ride a unicycle. Fortunately she already knows how to ride a bicycle. So as she learns, she can apply balance, pedaling and forward movement skills she already has. Now she has to get used to and apply backwards motion, the lack of handlebars and no brakes. She will continually apply what she knows, but success requires blending it with new techniques.

Knowledge of new concepts is strengthened with extended thoughts about the new skills and tasks. Reflection, experimentation and application send new concepts over into long-term memory. This is why training works better with less listening and more doing. Discovery exercises like situational analysis and case studies done in group scenarios help shuffle the information along in the brain where it can be easily accessed. It helps when students have to stop and think, and compare the gaps between what was familiar to them in the past and what they are being presented to use in the future.

Still, however, that is the classroom: How do we support students so they can access those fledgling memories and change their behavior in the job area?

In the Lean Manufacturing training scenario above, only the training session sounds like it went well. But did three people from the team all "need" to go, or was the burden placed on the rest of the team not worth it? Was developing Lean Manufacturing activities part of the site strategy? If not, that is further waste, as there is no alignment towards site goals, which often means a lack of support for training at the highest levels. Often training initiatives that are "nice to have" die an early death. This may happen due to a goal set by someone other than the direct manager to spread a new initiative, such as Lean Manufacturing in the organization. The leader may have agreed to send them at some less busy time in the past, but did not make plans with the students as to what they would do after the training. At this point, having the production area converted to a more efficient, less wasteful area seems to be low on her list of priorities.

Another problem with the scenario is that there was a disconnect between the class goals and the department goals. The supervisor of the area may have been looking for some development options for the three employees and settled on this class. She had not thought about what should happen after class, to actually have the newly trained students work to remove waste from her production area.

When an instructor opens a typical class, he or she may go around the room, asking students what they want to get out of the session. An instructor might fall over if they heard a response like:

"I'll be mastering process mapping so that I can go back and map the Heat Treatment process and cycle to look for the seven-forms of waste with two coworkers." They may be shocked that a student has a plan right away to use the skills as most will say: "I want to understand this," or "get a refresh on that."

The key difference is that this bright student has a plan, perfected by his equally prepared and savvy supervisor. They know what is needed to make changes in the business and knows that training provides the tools to conduct that change. With this statement the student also puts pressure on the course instructors to give him or her the exact learning needed to be able to perform those tasks successfully once out of the classroom. The on-the-job experience then gives the student the chance to gain reflection, problem solving, repetition and hands on practice so that they can go on to use the training materials successfully again and again.

Although this is the ideal scenario, there are a few typical obstacles that keep success in training from happening perfectly. One is the general disconnect between instructors and the leaders of the students. This can most easily be observed with the hiring of an outside training vendor.

Picture this: A vendor calls someone in Human Resources and pitches their Time Management class: "It's the next best thing to enhance productivity, returning rave reviews, a 300% return on investment for all kinds of companies, including your competitors!" In their opinion, we had better purchase this class before losing all our market share and face tanking the business due to slow and sloppy work habits. The Human Resources contact remembers a complaint in staff meetings about slow productivity and general poor response time from the Engineering group, and forwards the vendor's contact and pitch to the Director of Engineering. The director remembers an order from the general manager to focus on employee development planning. He figures the group could use some organization skills, and tells HR to set up the class. Two sessions are offered and most engineers and maintenance employees attend, learning new tips and tricks to organize their day. They return to work, having had a nice day, with catered food, long breaks and a chance to chit chat with their co-workers. The next day the director asks a few students about the class, they respond positively, that it was good, that they learned some new tips.[5]

Table 4.1 shows the percentage of expected or typical training results, which, according to research,[6] can be expected from an audience of 100 who attend a typical soft skills workshop:

Table 4.1

Learner Outcome	Percentage of learners who used none of the learned concepts at all	Percentage of learners who tried *some* new skills but gave up before they became a habit	Percentage of learners who used new skills and had a result that helped the business
Researched Percentage	~15%	~70%	~15%

Table 4.2 shows the typical reasons for failure. Notice the high percentages of failure with needs analysis and application.

Table 4.2

Failure Reason:	The training was not what the learners needed	The learning session itself was poor (Ineffective design)	Application environment (no leader support, no incentive)
Researched Percentage	~40%	~20%	~40%

As you can see from the results above, training is a multi-step process that needs specific attention in several areas to make it work. It may take some real creativity to plan actions for trainees to take after training, but it should coincide with the goals the business unit needs to achieve anyway. It is worth it to save that large percentage of students who are not using new skills on the job. We have put in too much time, effort and money in analyzing the need and designing the training to face that loss now.

Let's look at a more ideal scenario. Let's imagine that a new business priority is to start using Lean Manufacturing concepts in the production areas, starting with a deep housekeeping and a workspace chosen to act as a pilot, and so a supervisor partners with a small team to set up "6S training". The goal of the training is that each team member is taught to analyze and act on objects and pieces of equipment in the line (Sort, Set in Order, Shine, Standardize, Sustain, Safety).

Perhaps a person on the small team is a subject matter expert in Lean Manufacturing concepts. Fantastic. Another is in charge of work assignments for the trainees. Wonderful. Now we have to design a training program effectively so that the business can successfully launch their 6S effort.

So a business need has been identified and established. The entire team needs to transition their line into a 6S work area and make it stick, with complete ownership and maintenance of the 6S methodology so that it will be sustained into the future. The following chart shows an example of a high level plan starting with an example business need and ending with the instructional approach for learners. Notice, this is a truly hands-on approach, with a short introduction of each concept in the classroom, and before even one student has a chance to yawn hugely, they are whisked out of the classroom to the work area to apply what they have learned so that we are confident they have mastered each SMART objective. The business need: Start Lean Manufacturing by rolling out 6S.

The new behaviors that are needed are to transform the filling area into a 6S area, and add auditing steps to keep it sustained.

The needed skills and knowledge of the students: Identify and differentiate between each S in 6S (Sort, Set in Order, Shine, Standardize, Sustain, Safety).

A. Clean/re-paint objects and area to make it look new

B. Use color/labels to standardize pathways and objects

C. Analyze safety of each object and work practice

D. Design an audit to sustain new work practices

To meet the needs of the students, we plan lectures on each topic in the classroom, and a hands-on demonstration of each topic in the work area.

Moving from a short lecture in the classroom, then out to the floor to apply it, then back for a session about the next step and so on is a model that provides much of what the student needs to learn the concepts of deep organization and housekeeping from the inside out.

Post-Course Work-Designed Up Front

Did you notice the partnership between the expert instructor and the leader? They decided on a feasible plan together, with a hands- on experience for the trainees and a plan to follow up and gauge the success with the team weekly. Due to their control and oversight of the training design and the tasks performed afterwards, plus their commitment to having the project owned by the line team after the project end, we can predict a successful outcome. Theoretically. (If priorities change, people change jobs, or the line is significantly reconfigured due to changing production needs, then typically the effects of the training will erode). Now this partnership between the instructor and the leader can happen with an external vendor, but a close and sustained working relationship with meetings before and after the training sessions will help.

More Post Course Work for Individuals

How about planning ahead for a more effective learning experience with the employee? Here are a few ideas: Sending a student off to an expensive seminar? Give them assignments to do. It makes a sense. If you are sending students to courses, that should be linked to a need for the organization. Clarify with the student as to what that need is, and be sure they are clear on what the organization expects to get out of it. Table 4.3 has some ideas for deepening the impact of training:

Table 4.3

Sending an employee to Leadership Training?	A list of who they will coach, a new communication plan, a situational analysis of their team's development needs, and conflict resolution plan between two teams is due in a week
Going to Italy to visit an equipment designer?	Come back with troubleshooting guides, potential future upgrades, optimization tips and a draft implementation plan
Sending an employee to Train the Trainer class?	They will train three employees on technical topics within three weeks. The training plan and student feedback are then due to the leader
Sending an employee to a seminar about new technology?	The student will plan a synopsis and send it out with supplementary materials to the entire team, or make a presentation at a meeting.
Sending a student to become certified as an internal auditor?	Design an audit for the organization, complete with deeply diving questions, criteria for success and a prioritized audit plan.

What is Support and Reinforcement?

A learning process is a time to lower the consequences for mistakes for students. If the fear of failure is hanging over the heads of trainees, they tend to slow down and try less creative ideas. For example, when asking a learner to perform research and present options of new types of tooling upgrades for the production floor, have them present it first to you and other team members, not straight to the top of the Engineering department where their mistakes might get them shot down and demoralized. Stretching the neck out a bit at a time is better for learners. Be supportive when they slip up, as they are learning new skills, and have less judgment than they did before the mistake than they will have after it. Your aim is to build their awareness of the business, how to succeed in it and how to grow their judgment and decision making ability; in other words, to become more valuable to the organization.

"Just in Time" Training

Just-in-time training (JIT) refers to a purposeful reduction between the time of training and the time of application, and in some ways it is a combination of training and application. We have already discussed a way of doing that with the 6S training scenario. Part of the training is delivered just prior to doing the applicable work with the guidance of the expert, so the students are using the short lectures right away as they decipher the meaning of the content in the context of their own work area. As they toss out nearly empty duplicate bottles of spray cleaner and forgotten rusty tools in the bottom of drawers, and label clearly each cord, hose and lever, the students are seeing the results and the advantages of an organized work station. By the end of that training, and with the help of weekly audits, the team is very clear on the concepts, methods and maintenance of a 6S production line.

It is of great importance to shorten the time it takes between training and the application of training in the job. For example, the training period for new software should be just before implementation. If there is a last minute delay of the launch of the software, more practice sessions should then be scheduled so that the skills are there, ready to put in place when the old system is cut off. It is understandably difficult to add back into the project plan additional training sessions, on top of the delays that have already impacted the bottom line, however, it is not fair to expect students to retain the short-term skills they picked up in the classroom over weeks until the software rolls out.

The Typical Disconnect with External Training Providers

Organizations often pour out time and money to vendors who promise to deliver a high quality training program that will turn around lackluster performance. They might open the conversation with, "Can I have 20 minutes of your time to hear about your needs in leadership development?" If they can get your attention they will bring in a few "associate specialists" (sales persons) ask a few questions, make a few sympathetic comments and show case studies with huge return on investment for such large organizations as...just fill in the blank.

Some top leaders buy their solutions and somehow the fine print suggestions about the role the organization "should" play to get these results is missed. The communication and goal setting for front line leaders may be weak, progress checks drop off the agenda at high level meetings, and the re-enforcement of the changed behaviors does not seem to happen. And why would frontline leaders have an easy time with this? They were not part of the sales pitch or the decision to have this training, they were only told to send their people, reducing productivity numbers they may be held accountable to keep high. The culture has not told them to act to support training and re-enforce new behaviors in the past, and they are busy finding ways to make up for lost productivity. The training providers are not bad people; they are often excellent instructors, with experience and credentials. But they are not the people leaders, and have very little control of what happens after the students leave the classroom. The deep partnership that should be happening between leaders and instructors often does not develop. So much lost!

Requiring Students To Use the Training

When you thoughtfully send the right students to a class, also make sure they are ready to help solve business problems just afterwards. Plan the improvements they can make together and shout out the good news when problems are solved. The recognition for students is valuable to them, and don't forget to claim to your own applause for designing an effective training plan. In this list of actions taken following a class on best practices in pneumatics, these (fictitiously named) mechanics made modifications to production systems for measurable improvements:

1. Jan Brown-Replaced a ½ inch airline with a ¾ inch line, and installed a gauge to improve airflow and make it more consistent.

2. Kerry Green- Investigated and replaced airlines with brushes or closed systems on filling lines to save $5,475 per open line per year.

3. John Gray- Replaced incorrect fittings and performed a cleaning of the air lines on a production line resulting in increased RPMs on an air motor.

So beyond the measurable impacts soon after class, the students had the added benefit of lasting experience, permanent, and memorable accomplishment in the area of pneumatics troubleshooting and design.

The Critical Role of Leaders

So obviously a leader's action to enable learning is critical. Employees generally do what they are told. If they are not told explicitly to use new behaviors and given the chance and expectation to use them, producing a specific result, then it is hard on them to buck against the habits that may have formed over years. They also will need the understanding that they may be a bit slow at mastering the new skills in the beginning. Some employees may have their head whirling as they step out of a training class with fledgling skills and hope the leaders forget that they are expected to use them. Document that expectation and revisit it often and half the battle is won.

Wrapping up

Just a little summary of the science in this chapter: People need a chance take in, reflect on and introduce new skills and insights. Reinforcement, discussion and analysis of the concepts through exercises create new memories. When those memories are sufficiently developed through reflection and repetition, they transform from short-term to long-term memories in the brain. This is a key concept to return to, as it is important in transference of skills and knowledge into behavior on the job. In addition, the leader must help drive learning out of the classroom. Let's go back over some of the examples covered in the book so far to discover the effectiveness of training, in Table 4.4.

Table 4.4

Training Scenario	Business Need	Training Method	Leader Takes Action?	Result
Handling fragile probes Ch.1	Lower costs from probe replacements	Hands-on by manager	Involved team in monitoring	**Win: 2650% ROI**
Welder training Ch.1	Downtime and calls to the vender	Blended, classroom and at equipment	Directing team to use skills and monitoring	**Win: 400% ROI**
Preparing for Auditors - Ch. 3	Prepare workers to shine in audit	Fire hose method (ineffective)	None	**Loss: Poor audit results**
Lean Manufactur -ing -Ch. 4	Unclear	Engaging, well designed	None	**Loss: No use of training**
Time Management Ch. 4	Unclear	Engaging, well designed	None	**Loss: No use of training**
6S Training Ch. 4	Implement Lean tool in an area	Classroom and hands on training	Involved with ongoing audits	**Win: Reaches goals**

In what way will you support and re-enforce the use of training in a way that causes sustained behavior change? Turn to the worksheet to plan it out.

Chapter 5: Performance Management (or Superpower Development Plan)

A Standard Approach to Effective Training

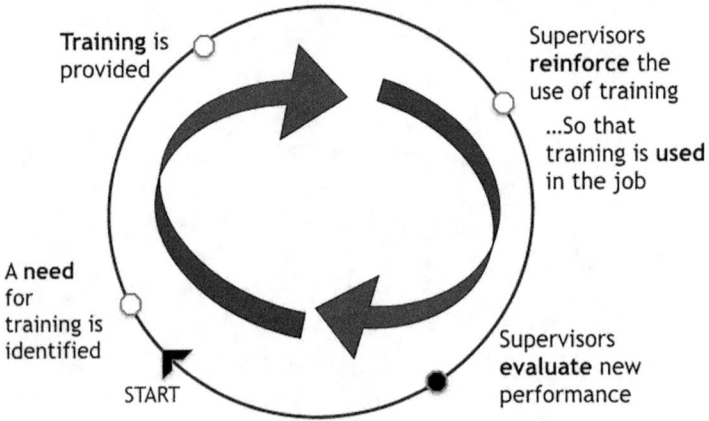

Training is provided

Supervisors **reinforce** the use of training

...So that training is **used** in the job

A **need** for training is identified

START

Supervisors **evaluate** new performance

Introduction

Performance Management is a yearly or semi-yearly evaluation of an individual's performance and a chance for the employee to know how they are doing. Most organizations in western civilizations have been serious for years about performing these evaluations. They provide a legal basis for employment decisions, such as promotions, raises and terminations. The feedback is important for employees so that they know performance matters, how to change for the better, and to plan the steps to get to higher performance. Some leaders consider them a waste of time, and see no benefit from the process. So let's call it something else entirely. How about the Superpower Development Plan (SDP)? Let's look at it this way: Performance management works when leaders are serious about getting the best from their workforce. Since you are reading this, let's assume that you are. Then you can look at the performance management process as a contract between yourself and your employee. Get agreement from your employee that he/she will get the objectives that you and they set together completed and that in exchange for that work, they themselves will learn new, valuable skills with your help. Call it a Bargain for Growth (B4G) or Employee Success Plan or anything else less boring than Performance Management, but use it as time carved out to create more value and effectiveness in employees through feedback and planning.

This Chapter Will Help You:

- Deepen the engagement of your employees through learning.
- Get the most of performance management sessions with employees.
- Get students on the hook to use new skills and improve their skills.

- Plan to move each employee up in the continuum of value and find your superstars.

Employee Engagement

Studies at the time of publish show that much of the workforce remains disengaged, meaning they are mentally checked out, hiding in plain sight, going through the motions, or actively trying to get out of the organization. Obviously there is a wide range within the "disengaged" label, with some employees mildly effected, and some seriously so. About 60% of managers answer to this description according to a late 2015 Gallup survey and nearly 70% for their subordinates.[1] In the wonderfully named *I Quit But Forgot To Tell You,*[2] one of the reasons an employee becomes disengaged is that their learning and development opportunities and activities have ended.

Learning and development opportunities are a huge motivator for employees and highly linked to engagement in the workplace. The Association for Training and Development published a survey of over 750 managers and executives of companies of 500 employees and larger. The top findings of factors impacting engagement were:

1. Quality of training/learning opportunities

2. Learning through stretch assignments

3. Frequency of training or learning opportunities

4. Breadth of training or learning opportunities

5. Leaders training in how to evaluate performance

6. Employee on-boarding processes[3]

Performance Management: Do We Gotta Do it?

Businesses do performance management differently, some on paper, others in fancy systems. Some link performance management to development goals, and some limit them only to business objectives to achieve. The biggest variable continues to be the quality of the feedback and the time taken in the busy world of business to delve deeply into the year over year achievement for the individual.

Interestingly, in the last few years, a small number of large and successful companies have eliminated a substantial piece of their performance management systems, including 6% of fortune 500 companies. Microsoft, Accenture, Adobe, Deloitte, Gap and Medtronic reduced the process and costly systems in favor of simplified, shorter, and more frequent feedback. The idea is: "Why keep a gargantuan, cumbersome system that pays us little back?"[4] It makes a certain amount of sense. If your company is hiring the right persons, and leading them the right way, then why do we need to force rank them, or document their weaknesses year after year?

Well, if your organization is not in that small, growing circle of companies, let's still get everything you can from the performance system you have: use it in a way to support outstanding growth and value for your employees. The difference of having superpower-developing perspective rather than as a policing critic is huge. Let's illustrate with a story.

Dale is a long-term employee who comes in to work on the edge of lateness and races his co-workers to the parking lot at the end of the shift. He mostly keeps his mouth shut in meetings except for the low-level, grumbling complaints he shares with his neighbors in the very back of the room. He has been disciplined for not filling out records correctly and often rolls his eyes when you, his leader, talk with him. He does the minimum and has an attitude to match. In his work area, there are 4-5 others like him, all seemingly checked out. As Dale's leader what are your choices?[5]

A. Kick him to the curb, and throw his grumble buddies out too, they do not deserve to work with your company, you'll squeeze Human Resources to replace them ASAP.

B. Have a coaching session on his attitude, tell him he must have a more respectful demeanor and stop grumbling during your staff meetings. If the disrespect continues he will likely only earn a "Meets Expectations" at his annual performance review.

C. Meet with Dale and discuss your concerns and ask to hear his. Ask for a reduction in hostility. If you are doing something to cause the hostility, require that he name it. Offer a partnership in putting his performance on an upward spiral and give him a chance to think about it. Meet often to make the plan a success. Treat the other low performers as separate and distinct opportunities for improvement.

Remember, people get more engaged when they are learning, and a big thrill for them may be to learning more about a topic and skill they are already interested in. And though options A and B might be the easiest, option C has the biggest chance of strengthening your team and improving your own leadership skills. The cost of replacing the typical employee can be up to approximately 1.5 times their annual salary according to Kabachnick[6], due to the time to search, interview and train new hires, and then, lost productivity and errors made by new learners in the role. Also, your own leader will see you more as a hero when you turn around performance problems.

The role of a performance management process also may be used as an incentive to hold employees accountable over learning plans. When you realize an employee is not able to perform all the facets of their job as compared to the job description (as in the example in Chapter 1, the woman who could not use a newer tracking system and left this work to others), this is the perfect time to let that person know, in the backdrop of a conversation about the needs of the organization. This is a formal chance to put an employee on notice that performance must change, skill gaps must be filled and to assign a date to have it accomplished.

In a busy environment, with an occasionally quick word in the hall between leader and employee, there is little time for feedback. If leaders wait for the end of year conversation to start a discussion about poor performance, the employee may be surprised, defensive and spend a long period in angry denial about their review. Negative feedback should be given more often, in a quiet, private area and it should target those behaviors and skill gaps that are a problem for the department and business. On the other hand, the positive behaviors and attributes that contribute success to the business can be in public (although it is always best to ask, as some do not like the spotlight). Either type of feedback of a significant nature should be documented.

Performance management conversations are a great time to assess the results of training you have assigned this person to accomplish, based on what was discovered during the needs analysis phase. If no real change happened for the employee (no higher level judgment or more advanced skills have been apparent to make improvements in the business), then take it as a shared responsibility and learn from the experience. Have a frank discussion with the employee: Were they given the right training? Recall their success in learning the concept. Did they have ample opportunity to use the new skills in the job? Try and pinpoint the exact breakdown.

Now, if priorities have changed, the needs have gone away, and classes were canceled mid-stream, it should not be a real surprise, and in no way a penalty to the employee. Priorities shift, hotter issues come up, and often it is learning that is displaced in favor of the new issues. But this is a short-term reprieve, right? Those issues may become hot again, so if these skills will still be needed, figure out a way to get it off the back burner and work in a plan to fill those gaps. If the employee did not bother to go to class, read the assignments, or do the assigned work, then this merits a stronger discussion, and consequences. Students simply must do their part, as they are being paid by the organization to bring value. It should be clear; are they an asset or a liability to the company?

Developing Your Team Through Delegation

Continuing the discussion about employees as assets, do you have a person who can adequately back you up when you are out? If so, where would you like to work with them to improve their judgment? Could they handle any of the crises that you regularly solve? Could that person improve their situational analysis and decision-making skills? Can they help keep conflict lower among the team? Are they ready for medium sized improvement projects?

Delegation is often an underused skill for leaders. Your author has heard the following laments:

- "I do not have time to hand hold one of my people, it would be faster and less risky to do it myself!"
- "My team is already working full speed, I do not have anyone who I can delegate to!"
- My best team members have made it clear, they do not want additional responsibility."

Although these may be seen as serious obstacles, it may just take a few conversations, a few instances of creative and positive coaching conversations and low-cost rewards and recognition (see how in Chapter 6), to change attitudes about being open to learning for the entire team. A few examples of positive spins are as follows:

- "Kelly, I feel you are ready for some more interesting work. I noticed you often think carefully through problems and offer ideas to modify the production line. Would you be interested in doing some investigation into the oil leaks we are noticing a few times per week? You might try picking the brain of the 2nd shift process engineer; she was working on the unit a month ago. You may be able to save us some downtime by collecting data and proposing a solution for the mechanic."

- "Hi Jackie, I just wanted to say, your idea to store all the acidic reagents in narrow shelves in this cabinet saved us time instead of searching for the right reagent in two locations. I was wondering if you could propose any other ideas to reorganize the lab so we can be more efficient? Could we meet on Friday to discuss what you have in mind?"

- "Ron you are the fastest with computerized systems and you make the fewest errors of the team. Could I rely on you to produce the draft production output report after checking for inaccuracies? I sure would feel better if you had a chance to check over the weekly inputs of the team before the numbers were due to the Director."

- "Ann, I have a minor mystery and I feel you are the right one to figure this out for the team. Every now and then a critical component is said to be in the system, but we cannot locate it, and it causes a major disruption about every three weeks. Can you

119

please investigate these last three incidents and decide on a procedure to stop the cause of this? I will have Sarah stand in for you while you do your fact checking and writing, just let me know when you need her. Have a draft procedure for me in two weeks that adds a safeguard so this cannot happen, we are really losing too much time for this issue".

Remember a few rules for delegation: Be very clear as to the deliverable, the completion date and the frequency. Is it a one time request or task, or is the expectation that it be repeated weekly? Also, make sure it is clear they own this task or topic, and are expected, once they agree, to deliver with your help and support. Support looks like this: check in at the frequency warranted by their experience. Be ready to offer advice if needed, remove obstacles and facilitate their success, while letting them do the task. For example, let's say Kelly, Jackie and Ron are entry level operators, on the job for less than a year each, fully familiar with the tasks and equipment for the job, but they have not had any delegation brought to them before. You probably will want to meet with them before, during and soon as after the task is done, give them feedback on their actions and decisions, ask them how they thought they did and discuss further tasks they can be assigned to. They have each learned to use their brain for something other than execute the job they already know, they are organizing, analyzing and finalizing data inputs with accuracy. In the fourth scenario, Ann has a higher level of complexity in her assignment and in creating a way to stop the future losses. She may have less than strong experience, so here is where the training comes in: She may need training in root cause analysis, testing the proposed outcome, and writing procedures, so she will need more support and check ins over the course of this project.

The goal with delegation is to get your employees comfortable taking on higher level tasks that increase and broaden their experience, build judgment and best of all, cause them to bring their brain to work. Employee involvement in solving the issues of the workplace can help significantly with engagement as well as providing improvements to the workplace.

Other ideas are to write standard procedures, do root cause analyses, develop subject matter experts, share knowledge through cross training, investigate missed orders, or examine worn parts and quality defects. Give them leadership experience by asking them to select and lead a small team. Remember to recognize those efforts, both with feedback, public thanks and through thoughtful evaluations during performance management.

Evaluating New Hires

New hires need much more frequent feedback. There is a higher failure rate for the newly hired employees, and it varies widely depending on the level of the position in the company.

Leaders have to expect that, that the people they hire will have varying skills. Some people do extremely well in interviews, making a quick, solid connection with the interviewer with a friendly and confident air. Often leaders go with the "gut feel" in an interview and hire the ones they like, but then find that the person struggles with mastering the databases, or in keeping up with the correct speed, or noticing the details of the process parameters, resulting in defects. The gut feeling is more about feeling connected with a person; it has little to do with skills and abilities.

The solution to a bad hire is to cut short the employment, though it may be tempting to see if the situation improves, or speculate that they may be better in another type of role and to "keep an eye out." But the truth is, a bad hire will likely be that way for the long term. Many employers use a probationary period to judge if the trainee is progressing as expected through the training period. Although it is a waste to terminate an employee, and go through the time and expense of filling that position again, it is also a poor deal for the company to undergo the losses that employee will incur by not earning the salary paid to him or her. In reality, poor performers lose the company money, and if the training has been consistently applied, yet has been ineffective, leaders have to make this hard choice.

Prevent Loss by Making the Right Hire

One of the best preventive steps is to use structured tools to evaluate candidates, such as validated skill tests (employment laws vary by country, so ensure you have an expert to advise you on how to set this up) and also a structured interviewing process, such as the Behavioral Event Interviewing. You may have been part of this type of interview yourself in the past. A typical question goes like this: "Tell me about a time when you proposed a business improvement and saw a measurable result? The interviewee is asked to give a specific situation, the action they took and the result. This goes with the premise that past actions in other jobs or situations can predict their future performance. If they have stories of their successes in past jobs that are similar to the behaviors and successes being looked for in the present job, well ding! ding! We may have found a winner. If they are straight out of school then this method is difficult, unless they have internship or community involvement type of experience. See the appendix for a list of typical Behavioral Event style questions.

Wrapping Up

Imagine if you could make an accurate estimate of your team's performance and determine that four of the ten are under-performers, five of the ten are average and one is exceeding your expectations. This roughly amounts to a loss for your company in performance. In other words, the four under performers are likely losing money for your company. Even the five at "meets expectations" could be doing better. What if you could reduce or eliminate that loss, raising standards for all so that you have a high-performing team? This past chapter is about determining the outcomes of development plans for the students, and effectively selecting team members into a team. But what if you have been assigned to a team that has a long history of *"We've always done it that way?"* And why would your new team go along with better performance if the rest of the departments were allowed to stay at the same level?

For a workforce, a broader view is needed, such as effective people policies, selection strategies, establishing a learning culture, and accountability for high skills, both for every individual and for leaders as well. Building a context for a high performing organization facilitates that transition. In the next chapter, we will explore the ways to position learning and performance as a business imperative, so that skill building, and high performance expectations become the norm.

Before we leave this chapter, check what the next steps are in the worksheet. There is space to record all of the levels of training effectiveness that we have discussed. Don't worry if you do not think you will have smoking gun data to show changed behavior has impacted the business, there may not be good value-linked data to measure this. Instead, less tangible benefits may be measured and documented, such as tardiness, employee satisfaction, or safety audits conducted. When you have data at any level, record it on the worksheet.

Chapter 6: Growing a Learning Culture

Introduction

Does your organization have a goal to improve performance overall? Is there pressure to be more agile, change-ready and resilient in the marketplace? Yet do training initiatives seem like too much work to get results? Is it difficult to engage owners to be responsible for supporting learning? To make it as easy as possible for learning to meet its mark and bring fast, sustainable change, set goals to grow a learning culture.

This Chapter Will Help You:

- Decide what modifications, communication, support, behaviors and actions are required to establish and deepen a "learning culture."
- Recognize indications of learning culture growth and those actions that stop it in its tracks.
- Stop trying to push a boulder up hill. Determine solutions to make learning snowball, picking up speed and size as it goes.

Training and Production Goals are Often at Odds

Some of the common obstacles to growing a learning culture are the sometimes invisible, built-in, systemic factors that compete with organizational learning. If leaders receive favorable performance ratings by ever increasing production rates and cost savings, they may anticipate a disadvantage when they think of sending their employees to training. If the organization has a history of only slowing production for mandatory training, which leaders see as a waste, it should be no surprise that leaders do not predict that training will necessarily help them achieve their goals of cutting costs and generating high production numbers. Remember that human beings tend to do what they are rewarded to do. Those incentives may be subtle and individualized, depending on their wants and needs, but people do respond to rewards.[1]

It is when the decision makers high in the organization begin adding training to the agenda, and change the rewards systems for leaders that a learning culture can start to get a foothold. The following story illustrates one such transformation.

Helping Leaders to be Accountable for Developing Employees

Once, years ago as an entry level department trainer in a huge manufacturing facility, my manager suddenly came into the office and started a conversation with "We have to pick some development classes for you! What do you want? Time Management? Or Communication Skills?"

I curiously asked what was wrong, has something changed? The manager replied with a slightly wild look in his eye: "We won't get our bonuses unless we develop everyone!" As he had a large team, it was easy to see he was overwhelmed and trying to simply check the box so everyone had a class to go to. The next year, leaders were more thoughtful, and assigning an employee to lead a cross functional team was popular, as well as creating ways to help groups to work better together and writing new standard procedures. Certifications were sought after, tuition assistance was added as a benefit, and the rewards and recognition system revolved around the accomplishment of learning. Over time, development planning improved, budgets and guidelines were better established and the organization started to realize the benefits through internal advancement for open positions. Soon it became obvious we were enjoying better retention of key talent. We also converted internal experts to instructors to share knowledge more effectively. Job ladders, a knowledge sharing repository and a simulation training area were created to great fanfare and visibility. After approximately three years, the use of learning as an every day part of business was successfully established. Granted, this was in a time where competition for skilled employees was fierce, and retention of key talent was a high priority. Regulatory agencies included a close look at training systems with every audit. This is why it was a brilliant move to get the manager's attention by shifting a focus to development planning and changing their reward system to support this business imperative.

Building a Learning Culture-In Your Department, or an Entire Organization

First take stock: Is learning happening irregularly, or only for mistakes? Are new hires left to "sink or swim?" Are processes performed inconsistently, with few employees highly skilled? Is there a low level of internal promotions? Are training results ever measured beyond Level 1 (the smile sheet)? Is development planning for individuals part of the performance management process, and if so, is the practice actually applied? Are leaders rated on their activities and success regarding their employees' development?

An excellent tool to do this learning culture assessment was published by in the Harvard Business Review[2]. It is a tool that employers can use to get an assessment of their own organization, and compare it to other like organizations. In large companies, the degree of learning support may vary widely, so this tool can be applied to individual departments and teams, and the results analyzed for the organization as a whole or by segment to see where improvements might make the biggest impact (find the link to this article and how to get the survey in the notes section).

The authors found the three key factors to focus on to build learning organizations are:

1.   A supportive learning environment

2.   Concrete learning processes and practices

3.   Leadership that reinforces learning

Influencing Leaders by Speaking Their Language: Converting Leaders to Allies

In some organizations, and in the minds of many leaders, learning as a business initiative is a tough sell. Some see it as purely a "warm and fuzzy, nice to have, we can do it when we have time," sort of after thought. In fact, training resources and budgets are generally the first to go in an economic downturn. One leader had directly told me. "Training does me no good! I've never seen a favorable result," with other leaders nodding around the table. With further discussion, we found some likely reasons and soon, they were interested, even excited about putting together a learning plan with the elements to make sure it returned a measurable investment.

One stellar way to show an organization where faith in training is low, is to show with credible data that learning initiatives turned a business problem around. One priority should be to gather a few great case studies; of defects reduced, customer loss averted, market share increased, money saved or gained, retention raised, or internal promotions increased. These are the sort of solutions leaders are looking for, and the more focus there is to solve real business problems, the more "warm and fuzzy" top leaders will feel about helping to raise the momentum by further supporting the learning and development efforts in the organization. Give them explicit "wins" with training. Where possible, show the organization that the headaches that they used to have that have vanished due to effective training. This will then generate more support, more attention and more credit given for learning as a business solution. See another example of a case study that measures the results of training in Appendix D. Notice how it measures every one of Kirkpatrick's levels of effectiveness and also measures return on investment.

What Does a Healthy Learning Culture Look Like?

Successful learning organizations treat skill and knowledge building as a natural extension of working. Leaders are measured in their development efforts for their people. The competition between reaching organizational goals and taking the time and effort to build the skills and abilities of employees is reduced, and rather, time for learning and development is budgeted for and integrated into the business model. Employees are encouraged to step up as Subject Matter Experts and share their knowledge. Willing employees are trained as instructors and assigned to teach others.

The rewards for fostering a learning culture are many. Such as organizational agility, internal promotions, lowered turnover, a performance improvement focus, a healthy succession plan, strength through cross training, a more engaged workforce, and less erosion after training. The behaviors that cause and sustain a learning culture must be embraced at the front line leadership and manager level for the culture to shift and allow learning to make its impact.

Leaders as Drivers of Learning

The importance of the involvement of the direct leader cannot be overemphasized. As we saw in the beginning of Chapter 4, it is not typical to have employee grab up all the learning opportunities they can and master them on their own initiative in the workplace, although it does happen, and these stars are likely going to shine with or without your help, because they are intentional about getting better every day. The other, approximately 85% need your help.

One young supervisor of the author's acquaintance had been one such self-driven employee, and worked his way up from a top Machine Operator to an assignment as a Department Trainer, and then was snapped up as a Supervisor on the night shift. Having been the type to "learn his lessons" and seeking out new skills and knowledge to help himself advance, he recognized right away that his new team needed better foundational skills- and slowed production to accomplish this. This was a huge risk, and went against the norm in an organization that struggled to place training on the agenda, let along putting it first. The new leader worked with employees on all the skills that were holding them back prior to his assignment, attacking knowledge gaps of system functions, and raising skills in mechanical troubleshooting. He explained himself to the students, encouraged them, and cajoled them into signing up for voluntary certifications to improve their skills farther.

When the new leader's director started to apply some heat to attempt to turn his attention back to "making the numbers," he asked for patience and a bit more time and explained what he was trying to do. Soon the productivity numbers started a slow change. Not letting up with skills, and making each problem a "learning moment" for his team, the night shift began to attract attention, as productivity numbers edged to new heights. Within three months of his assignment to the third shift, there was a startling and sustained difference in the number of units and equipment uptime on his shift, and his unit director was singing his praises as someone who succeeded in a tough environment, using *learning* of all things, even in the face of pressure from himself to stop and get back to putting out the units. That new leader's career has changed twice again for the better since this evidence of success using training, and the prediction is that he will continue to get top performance from his employees by helping them to reach high level skills.[3]

Let's Talk About Risk

A team is not working well together: Common activities are finger pointing, excuses, a lack of initiative and a low-level of participation in meetings. Absenteeism is trending higher in the ten-person department, leading to increasing complaints about workload. Communication between team members has slacked off, leading to incidences of confusion, duplicate work, and increasing hostility. The director of the unit has advised you, the new manager, to solve it and suggests a team building session including a discussion on personality styles and something to help the group work together better, topped off with a feel-good cookout on the back patio.

Although you are a somewhat new manager, and a transfer from another division of the company, you have your doubts that this would fix the situation, and decide do some deeper analysis before presenting your plan. You take a close look at the team's production output over the last year and sure enough, there is a downward trend in total output and machine uptime. This coincides with the time the previous manager left the organization, three months prior. Informal perspective gathering interviews reveal the following information:

- From a manager of another part of the unit: The previous manager, Dillon, was let go due to a serious incident resulting in a large amount of defective product that could not be reworked. It was nearly released and would likely have resulted in a product recall.

- From a mechanic: The machine technicians are not even trying to make adjustments anymore when there are minor stops. Instead, techs call the mechanics for every little thing, losing machine up time and preventing the maintenance department from sticking to their preventative maintenance schedule.

- From your own direct observation: Jerry, Darryl, Sophie and Marnie stand apart. These four seem somewhat surly, doing the minimum and keeping mostly out of sight. They can be seen often together on breaks, but they seldom mix with the rest of the team.

- From the Quality Manager: The incident from three months prior, resulting in the extensive product defect was thoroughly investigated. The root cause was a modification made to a raised pump platform in a mezzanine. Dillon had assigned a team of four to determine a way to reduce the amount of noise coming from the pump, as it had been increasing over time and was now close to the limit for allowable decibels for safe, sustained work exposure. The team changed the plate and the anti-vibration mat the pump was mounted on, which they found in a dismantled production line and put it back into service. Although the noise was reduced, the plate and mat were very old, and flakes of metal and crumbs of rubber came down in periodic showers, and were introduced as the components were added in the compounding step to the next four batches. The contamination was not noticed until the finished goods samples were analyzed.

Next you meet privately with the four techs involved. You start with a few statements about your resolve to help restore the team to the levels they used to achieve for productivity and team effectiveness and hope they can help you understand what has been happening lately. The group shrugs, but Sophie meets your eye. She discusses the incident and how the whole unit felt it was their fault Dillon was fired. He was a popular manager, and just wanted them to gain new skills with problem solving assignments. He was busy with new hires the day they were ready to implement their solution, so they did not discuss their "find" of the older plate and mat but went ahead with the change out, then reported that they had now a decibel measurement of 75 instead of the former 88. When the source of the quality defects were found, Dillon took full responsibility and lost his job. Darryl, Marnie and Jerry join in now with bitterness. The four resolved they would not be raising their hands for stretch assignments and discussed the "blindness" of upper management, the unfair treatment of employees and the uselessness and risk of making modifications. What will be your plan to remedy the problem? Is it a training problem?[4]

Actually, aren't there two problems? The first is to manage the expectations of the director who expects a team-building event and may actually be looking forward to dusting off a few old jokes and grilling some hotdogs for the team in the employee patio. The second is repairing the damage made to the learning culture of the department and the entire unit by this incident, and return productivity to former levels.

Here are a few ideas for how to proceed if a case like this falls into your lap. Assure your new boss that you have some ideas to change the business problems you have noticed, including lowered productivity, communication and absenteeism and that you would like to work with individual team members first with some feedback and coaching to get to know the team more and better understand their individual needs, aspirations and obstacles. And you would love the team building and hotdog feast and you think it would be a great kickoff to the upcoming holiday and annual company shut down in five months. Now that this is addressed, you can get down to the business of building trust, gauging development needs, and guiding the employees back to confidence in solving minor stops, investigating problems and participating in general improvements. A high level of judgment in your team is a goal worth working towards!

Are you starting to see how the past reactions to risk contribute to a culture about learning? According to research, learners need to feel safe to ask questions, try new ways of working, own up to mistakes and speak up to present an alternate viewpoint. If they are shut down more often then not and otherwise experience negative backlash for their learning efforts, then this will likely have a lasting effect in the wrong direction.[5]

Beyond a supporting learning environment, knowledge also has to "flow" in an organization. Knowledge has to move where needed, effectively and in a timely manner, in time to react to new organizational threats, and in order to proactively be ready for planned business changes as well. Of course, leaders need to recognize and start learning and development initiatives as a solution, and once this identification has occurred, the cycle described in this book must be applied to generate the results needed to support the organizational goals.

To this end, leaders must be involved, even if there is a Learning and Development Specialist, Manager, Consultant, Director, or a whole fleet of instructional resources. The leader will see more success with training if they are highly informed, visible and attuned to the learning process. Only the direct leader assigns work, can arrange a back up resource to cover while a learner is practicing or benchmarking, or reading or attending a class. Only direct and manager level leaders can budget time and money for training and fight to keep that budget when it is on the chopping block. Only leaders can encourage, support and give direction to their learners, so as to bring them up from their possible negative experiences with learning in the past and explore their high potential, exciting futures.

Here is a best-case scenario for building a learning culture. It cannot happen over night, but can move along, like a paper boat in a stream. Sometimes it may be caught up in some debris and take on water, but can be rescued and set upright again, gaining speed as obstacles are removed.

- The clear, visible and demonstrated support by top leaders, such as successful budgeting of funds, assigned subject matter experts to help design and support effective training, and the expectation and measurement of training effectiveness.
- Meeting agendas should include actions to monitor and evaluate training. (Not just "I've been told the students loved the class" because this is not necessarily compelling information for the organization.)
- A solid, measurable, development planning process, linked to the performance management cycle. Are leaders doing a good job with

development? Are development plans "SMART?" Are plans actually being completed with success, and has performance improved?

- Make learning and development projects and programs visible. Are their outcomes publicized? Are best practices shared? Can other groups and departments find out about learning successes and replicate them?

- Is there a goal set for a strong pipeline of "ready to advance leaders?" Is succession planning doing the job to provide replacements for key personnel as their positions become available? Is there a goal for internal promotions, versus filling key jobs from the outside?

- Is learning part of the current organizational goals, and if so, do employees at all levels know how they can support them?

The Rewards

Do you remember the story in Chapter 1 about the students who attended a safety class meant to educate students on the basic safe work practices, while their ways of working were subtly rewarding them to take shortcuts, bypass safety practices and otherwise put production first? This subtle reward system is replicated in countless ways in many parts of the working world, and indeed, is often what makes organizations function. Some leaders may expressly or subtly say to their team "I do not have much time to coddle you." Another is "Mistakes will cost you, personally" and there is "I do not have time for endless questions."

These messages introduce new employees to a culture that does not support learning, and in fact, starts to put ideas such as "mistrust, hide errors, and struggle in silence" into the minds of trainees. Here are some steps you can take as a leader to encourage learning in your area:

- Praise employees for learning new skills, gaining new educational milestones, and for sharing learning and advancing internally.
- Have conversations more often about development needs and planning with your team members (do not wait until the formal Performance Management Session.)
- Think about creative stretch assignments, and communicate them not as extra work, but as valuable opportunities for team member, and a reward for competence in the past.
- Support your team members as they learn: act as a buffer reducing the risk of damaging failures.

Think seriously about the "superpowers" than can be developed in your team. Give employees a reason to learn and a path on which to shine.

Fire-Fighting Mode

Obviously, a balance must exist between the proactive and the reactive work so that business can run, be profitable and yet reduce the time spent in "fire-fighting mode." Rework, finding lost materials and merchandise, paying for workman's compensation, losing customers to quality issues, all must be prevented by proactive work. For example, root cause investigations, goal-setting with employees, process mapping, designing training materials, and individual feedback sessions are some of the proactive tasks that take time, but they should eventually reduce the firefighting. As processes are brought into control, it grows easier to support a learning organization. Have you heard of the expression, "Work smarter, not harder?" This is what working proactively is all about.

Internal Promotions

What happens when employees move up from the inside? All sorts of wonderful things: Trust and loyalty increase, not only for the person promoted, but with the peers as well (hopefully the person had clear competencies needed for the job and was not a blood relative or in-law of the decision-maker). When top employees get a sense they are going somewhere in the company, they are more likely to hang in there and ride it out, brushing off requests to work for other splendid and quickly promoting companies. Your company benefits from a strong succession plan, and stability in the workforce, and the bonus of knowing the track record for the promoted employee. Let's say their records show that the promoted internal candidate had three years of "Exceeds Expectations" ratings and successfully completed all development plans. What do they have for external candidates? Perhaps a resume crafted by a hired expert, and references from an out of work roommate and Uncle Harold.

In fact Rioux & Bernthal found a failure rate of just 14% for internally filled job positions while there was a failure rate of 22% for external job hires.[6] The hint is that the internal candidate came up from a position of lesser authority, and responsibility. There is often less chance of promotion when jumping ship as recruiters do not like much risk, and will pick the candidate with as close as possible the experience level needed in the job. External hires are probably making a parallel transition for a similar level job and *still* failing at higher rates. This speaks loudly to the business advantages of purposely and effectively cultivating a learning culture, which expects and enables employees to move up in the organization.

Wrapping Up

Your last assignment on the worksheet is to start analyzing your organization's current state as a learning organization and your thoughts on deepening it. Set reasonable goals. As Rome wasn't built in a day, neither can attitudes change quickly about actively promoting learning as a business priority.

Congratulations! You now know much more about performance than the average person and, if you downloaded the performance plan and worked through it, you are well on your way to enabling a substantial change for the better for your employees and the organization. One last run through the cycle of effective training: To show superhero results through people, prevent waste in human performance interventions by sending people to the right training to impact their skill gaps, give them or insist on effective, engaging training with evidence of learning, follow learners out of the classroom and monitor and enable their use of new skills, and discuss the results of the new skills with the learners and set new development plans. Now report the changes that effective training has brought to the business and bask in the praise for fixing troublesome, stubborn organizational problems! Download another plan at www.BuildingGiants.com and do it again!

If this seems very difficult and time consuming, you are not the only leader or training professional who has felt this way. You can get help from industrial psychologists, partnership with local community colleges, and by developing helpful and expert instructors from within your own organization. Most of all help influence your top leaders by discussing your plans and asking for their support to remove obstacles. You are welcome to ask questions, learn more and share your outcomes at www.BuildingGiants.com and be sure to check out the additional tools and information in the Appendix section!

Appendix A: Creative Training Techniques

The Great Egg Drop

This exercise works great after some kind of self-discovery. Use it after a discussion of personality styles, team leadership training, or for as a team building event.

Divide a class into groups of at least three, preferably more. Tell them their objective: to construct a capsule with a raw egg using only the materials you supply and to drop it from a second story balcony (or in a pinch, toss each capsule over a fence).

Provide to each team: One raw egg, three paper towels, about a yard of string, two paper or Styrofoam cups, and a yard of tape (masking tape or blue craft tape).

Give them 5 minutes to construct their pod and choose a name for it. Meanwhile walk around and observe. Notice the team building, personality styles, or leadership actions for the debrief later.

Drop the eggs team by team and check the results!

Debrief: How did it go, what behaviors were observed? Reinforce main points, point out leadership behaviors, personality styles and ask for perspectives from students.

Get Acquainted BINGO

This is a great exercise for newer teams. Explain the rules to participants. They are looking among the group for people who match the descriptions and can sign their box. Each group member can only sign another person's bingo card a maximum of two times, but they can sign twice on as many cards as they like.

You may choose to make a time limit or encourage the group to go for a "blackout" by trying to get every box signed. This works well over a networking event or in an evening get together.

Offer fabulous prizes for a "BINGO" signatures across, down, or diagonally, and a grand prize for a blackout. Download the card at www.BuildingGiants.com.

Get Acquainted Bingo- rules: fill boxes with /initials (not more than 2 from each participant. A row across, down, or diagonally is a bingo, keep going until someone says Bingo)

Has an antique from any war	Is an only child	Has been skiing, or snow tubing	Has children	Does volunteer work
Reads the news every day	Has appeared on TV, radio, YouTube or on Stage	Worked for their organization for over 12 years	Has been to a concert in the last year	Likes to play golf (at least two times per year)
Knows someone famous (TV, Movies, Radio, web viral, or politics)	Has won a prize in the last year	Has found an arrowhead	Has a dog or a cat	Likes to play soccer (at least two times per year)
Has been to a movie in the past month	Enjoys camping (at least once per year)	Has broken two bones	Has been on a cruise	Has jumped out of an airplane.
Has had a pet fish, rabbit, turtle, lizard, snake, or tarantula	Runs in races or marathons	Can move one eyebrow	Has had a ride in a hot air balloon	Has traveled to Europe or Asia

Appendix B: Tools to Measure Level 1 and Level 2 Effectiveness

Go to www.BuildingGiants.com for the downloadable forms.

Level 1-Smile Sheet

Name of Trainer: Topic:

Please comment- what could have gone better?

What were some of the best parts?

Please rate the following from 5 to 1: (5 is strongly agree, 1 is strongly disagree)

The presenter was well prepared and organized   5 4 3 2 1

The instructor taught in a logical and clear manner   5 4 3 2 1

The information could be seen and heard clearly   5 4 3 2 1

My questions were answered adequately   N/A 5 4 3 2 1

Comments are appreciated! Thank you.

Level 2- Pre and Post Assessment

Pre-Post Assessment		
Take a Guess	The Question	Final Answer
1. d	EXAMPLE: What does level 2 evaluation of training measure? a. Student satisfaction b. Student learning c. Students use of new knowledge and skill on the job d. The impact of training on the business	1. b
2.		2.
3.		3.
4.		4.
5.		5.

Pre/Post Assessment Topic_____

Student Name (printed)_____

Student (signed)_____Date_____

Appendix C-Example of an Effectiveness Report

Leaders: Have you wondered what kind of information to ask of your instructors, Learning and Development Professionals or Human Resources after training? Read to the end and then you decide which of these 5 training effectiveness reports you would prefer.

A large manufacturing company assigned an internal expert to conduct Train the Trainer certification courses for 24 prospective internal instructors with the plan that they would spend a portion of their time as trainers in the subjects in which they are highly competent. The instructor is to report on the effectiveness of the class after 3 months. Which report would get the most favorable attention from upper management?

After the class, the Train the Trainer instructor submits the following report:

Potential Report #1:

"It was my pleasure to teach the students Train the Trainer techniques! They were a very lively bunch and seemed to enjoy themselves. They rated the class at 4.5 on a 5 point scale overall. All 24 students indicated they plan to conduct training for others

152

in the next few months, and that this class helped them to feel prepared.

Potential Report #2:

"It was my pleasure to teach the students Train the Trainer techniques!

1. They were a very lively bunch and seemed to enjoy themselves. Students had a high level of satisfaction about the class: Overall rating was 4.5 on a 5 point scale. Key comments were misgivings about being assigned as a trainer due to workload and preference (three students).

2. I reviewed each plan throughout the day, the students were corrected and coached the most on forming SMART objectives, and planning activities to evaluate the attainment of training objectives. Each student left the class with an effective training plan.

Potential Report #3:

"It was my pleasure to teach the students Train the Trainer techniques!

1. Satisfaction: (As above)
2. Learning: (As above)

3. Use of learning in the job: By the deadline, (3 weeks post class) 14 students (60%) had executed their training plan and turned in student feedback sheets. The student feedback sheets indicated their new instructors had used the structure taught them, including:

a. Establishing credibility

b. Expressing expectations for students in the form of SMART objectives

c. Effectively demonstrating the task or topic

d. Using creative training techniques to let students apply concepts

e. Evaluating skills and knowledge

Potential Report #4:

It was my pleasure to teach the students Train the Trainer techniques! The following impacts as a result of the class were measured:

1. Satisfaction: (As above)

2. Learning: (As above)

3. Use of Learning: (As above)

4. Effect on the business. In the next three months, the following reports were collected:

    a. Student one shortened changeover time through training for three lines, saving an average of 230 minutes per day.

b. Student four improved component flow by training others on standard work, reducing late deliveries to the department by 15%.

c. Student eleven devised a new color based sorting system for waste and trained all workers to use it and monitor its use for errors. Time to sort was reduced by 30%, and overall waste for the plant was reduced by 9%.

d. Student seventeen created a gauge-training cart, and left it in each line area for two days for self-training and practice, returning for an assessment for each operator. Gauge errors on first piece and periodic monitoring were reduced from 3.1% to 0.4% over three months.

Potential Report 5:

It was my pleasure to teach the students Train the Trainer techniques! The following impacts as a result of the class were measured:

1. Satisfaction: (As above)
2. Learning: (As above)
3. Use of Learning: (As above)
4. Effect on the business and financial impact. In the next three months, the following reports were collected:

Student one shortened change-over time through training for three lines, saving an average of 230 minutes per day, a financial impact of $170,000 per year.

Student four improved component flow by training others on standard work, reducing late deliveries to the department by 15%, a financial impact of $87,000 per year.

Student eleven devised a new color based sorting system for waste and trained all operators to use it and monitor its use for errors. Time to sort was reduced by 30%, and overall waste for the plant was reduced by 9%. A financial impact of $67,000 per year in reduced recyclable waste mixed with landfill waste.

Student seventeen created a gauge training cart, and left it in each line area for two days for self-training and practice, returning for a stringent assessment for each operator. Gauge errors on first piece and periodic monitoring were reduced from 3% to 0.4% over 3 months. A financial impact of $354,000 per year in reduced defects and scrapped lots.

5. Return on investment (ROI)

Cost of training: $12,000 for Train the Trainer class costs, salaries of experts and participants. Add an additional $21,000 for the time, materials and preparation of the four students who reported gains above (total $23,000).

Realized gain for 4 students who measured outcomes: $678,000

$$\frac{\$678,000-\$23,000}{\$23,000} \times 100 = 2847\% \text{ ROI}$$

Barriers:

Several barriers were recorded for students during subsequent interviews after the course and during the execution of training plans.

- Students disagreed with the assignment to train others; it was not in their comfort zone or career goals to take on the role alongside their already busy schedule (3 students).

- Students found when they returned to the job their priorities had been changed by their direct management, (6 students) while another student left the company before executing her plan.

- Some students noted a lack of authority over those they were assigned to train, and had difficulty being taken seriously by peers.

Enablers

Students noted the following actions that helped during the execution of training plans.

- The award of an internal certification made some students motivated to execute their plans.
- The report of their successes with training in their departments gave them pride and motivated others to reduce costs with training
- Being invited to leadership meetings to report on the effects of their training class helped students understand they were appreciated, and gave others an interest in joining a future class.

Recommendation:

It is your instructor's recommendation that students are nominated to attend future TTT classes based on high performance and expertise, time in the job to incorporate training others, and having a particular training project in mind when preparing to attend class to maximize return on investment.

Author's note: I challenge you to get a report on training effectiveness that is meaningful and actionable! (Maybe not every time, or even most of the time: let's face it, this takes resources, but at least for the critical, highly visible projects, to prove your effectiveness and to show the work of training and development initiatives!

Appendix D: Behavioral Interview Question Ideas

Ideally, you use behavioral interview questions in order to get a peek at a candidates' ways of working through stories of their past successes and errors. Tell the candidate that you are looking for answers that describe a task or incident, they action they took, and the results. If one part of their answer is missing, such as the exact action they took, or the outcome, come back to it and ask for that part.

Please discuss a time when you were assigned to work with someone with a forceful personality. How did you succeed?

Tell me about a time when you had a great idea and pushed through obstacles to see it succeed.

Tell me about a time when you solved a problem with creativity.

Tell me about a time when you improved the performance of your direct reports through development planning.

Describe a time where you had to influence a leader at a higher level than yourself.

Tell me about an error you made and what you learned from it.

Tell me about a time when you had difficulty with a change.

Tell me about a time when you helped reduce hostility or tension within a team.

Chapter Notes

Back Cover:

Wizeman, L.. Mckeon, Greg (2010, May). Managing yourself: Bringing out the best in your people. *Harvard Business Review.*

Preface:

1. ATD's State-of-the-Industry-Report (2013, Dec.) $164.2 Billion spent on training and development by US companies. https://www.td.org/Publications/Blogs/ATD-Blog/2013/12/ASTD-Releases-2013

2. In addition, see
    http://www.nwlink.com/~donclark/hrd/trainsta.html#transfer for more information and clarity on Training Transfer for a taste of the conflicting stories of how well training really impacts the bottom line.

3. Rynes, S. L., Giluk, T. L., & Brown, K. G. (2007). The very separate worlds of academic and practitioner periodicals in human resource management: Implications for evidence-based management. *Academy Of Management Journal,* 50(5), 987-1008

4. Burke,L.,Hutchins, H. (2007, September).Training transfer: an integrative literature review. *Human Resource Development Review* Vol. 6: 263-296.

Chapter 1: Failures in Training Can Hurt Your Business

1. Sue is fictitious.

2. Dean, A., (2010, April) Employee training: Do it and prove it. *Peoria Magazines,* Inter business Issues.

3. Shaw, E. (1995, April) The training-waste conspiracy. *Training,* v32 n4 p59-60,62,64-65

4. Kirkpatrick D.L. (1959). Techniques for evaluating training programs. *Journal of American Society of Training Directors.* 13 (3): pp21–26

5. Kirkpatrick, D.L., & Kirkpatrick, J.D. (1994). Evaluating training programs, Berrett-Koehler Publishers San Francisco.

6. Kirkpatrick, D.L. (1998). Another look at evaluating training programs. Alexandria, VA: *American Society for Training & Development.*

7. Philips, J., Stone, D. (2002) *How to measure training results: A practical guide to tracking the six key indicators.* McGraw Hill, New York.

8. A true story in a money-loss situation, where a credible subject matter expert who was also in a leadership role applied simple training principles in partnership with the Learning and Development Manager, and with reinforcement and monitoring saw a return on investment.

9. A true story of an effective partnership with a subject matter expert, also published previously on www.buildinggiants.com.

Chapter 2: Let's Identify the Need

1. Not a true story, but a typical scenario where unexplained problems are first tossed into the "Training Bucket" for resolution.
2. From personal experience-far too much time spent on the phone with far too many customer service agents.
3. This story is not based on any particular person, but all elements have been observed multiple times in dozens of scenarios.
4. Just an illustration, not based on a true scenario.
5. Levitt, Steven D.; Dubner, Stephen J. (2006).   William Morrow
6. Bodek, Norman, 2004 *Kaikaku* PCS Press, Vancouveer, Washington
7. A real incident witnessed by the author.
8. Hiatt, Jeffrey M., Creasey, Timothy J. (2012) *Change management: The people side of change.* Prosci Inc.
9. Kabachnick, T., (2006) *I Quit But Forgot to Tell you.* The Kabachnick Group, Key Largo, FL
10. Burt, C. (2015,May)A model of new employee safety risks. New Employee Safety, pp. 1-7

11. Adapted from author's Train the Trainer class-What not to do in On The Job Training.

12. Brydges, R., Nair, P., Ma, I., Shanks, D., & Hatala, R. (2012). Directed self-regulated learning versus instructor-regulated learning in simulation training. *Medical Education*, 46(7), 648-656.

13. For more information on simulation training methods and facilities, check www.BuildingGiants.com for future publications.

14. For more information on selection testing, become familiar with the Uniform Guidelines on Employee Selection and hire an expert (preferably an Industrial/Organizational Psychologist) for guidance.

15. To see the full case studies follow this link on the ACT WorkKeys website: http://www.act.org/workforce/case/

16. True story of a large waste in training.

17. Shaw, E. (1995, April) The training-waste conspiracy. *Training*, v32 n4 p59-60,62,64-65

Chapter 3: Training Designed for Success

1. This scenario was a true story of a failure of a company to prepare employees for encounters with audits, witnessed by the author.

2. Pike, R. W., (1994) *Creative training techniques handbook: Tips, tactics, and How-To's for delivering effective training.* (2nd ed.)Lakewood Books, Minnesota

3. See instructions for the great egg drop in the appendix section.

4. Andrade, J. (2010), What does doodling do?. *Applied Cognitive Psychology.* 24: 100–106. doi: 10.1002/acp.1561.

5. Hiatt, J, Creasey, T. 2012 Change management: *The people side of change.* Prosci.

6. Warr P, Allan C. (1999, September) Predicting three levels of training outcome. *Journal Of Occupational & Organizational Psychology*; 72(3):351-375

Chapter 4: Changing Behavior After Training

1. Fictional Illustration

2. Image redrawn by Jason Caselli, adapted from image in Dreams: Working Words of Wit and Wisdom, by Robert W. Pike. Used with permission.

3. Baldwin,T., Ford,K. (First published online, 2006, Dec) Transfer of training: A review and directions for future research. *Personnel Psychology. (41:1. p63-105)* March 1988. also Shaw, E. (1995, April) The training-waste conspiracy. *Training,* v32 n4 p59-60,62,64-65.

4. Schunk, D.H. (2012) *Learning Theories, an Educational Perspective.* Pearson. Boston, MA

5. Fictional illustration.

6. Brinkerhoff, R.O.,(2006) *Telling training's story*, Berrett-Koehler Publishers, San Francisco.

Chapter 5: Performance Management (or Superpower Development Plan)

1. Adkins, A. July 9, 2015 Gallup poll: Employee engagement unmoved in June. Retrieved from: http://www.gallup.com/poll/184061

2. Kabachnick, T., (2006) *I Quit But Forgot to Tell you*. The Kabachnick Group, Key Largo, FL

3. Paradise, A., (2008, January,) ASTD employee engagement study, 2007: Learning influences engagement. *T and D Magazine.* p 54.

4. Cunningham,L., (2015, July) In big move, Accenture will get rid of annual performance reviews and rankings. *Washington Post. Retrieved from* http://www.washingtonpost.com/blogs/on-leadership/wp/2015/07/21/in-big-move-accenture-will-get-rid-of-annual-performance-reviews-and-rankings/

5. Dale is fictional.

6. Kabachnick, T., (2006) *I Quit But Forgot to Tell you*. The Kabachnick Group, Key Largo, FL

Chapter 6: Growing a Learning Culture

1. Levitt, Steven D.; Dubner, Stephen J. (2006). *Freakonomics: A rogue economist explores the hidden side of everything.* William Morrow.

2. Garvin, D.A., Edmondson, A.C., & Gino, F.(2008, March). Is yours a learning organization? *Harvard Business Review.* https://hbr.org/2008/03/is-yours-a-learning-organization

3. True story, witnessed by the author.

4. A fictional story along with names of those involved.

5. Garvin, D.A., Edmondson, A.C., & Gino, F.(2008, March). Is yours a learning organization? *Harvard Business Review.* https://hbr.org/2008/03/is-yours-a-learning-organization

6. Rioux, S., & Bernthal, P. (1999). Succession management practices report. Pittsburgh, *PA:*Development Dimensions International

Selected Bibliography

Achor, S. (2010). *The happiness advantage: The seven principles of positive psychology that fuel success and performance at work.* Crown Publishing Group. USA.

American Psychological Association. (1954). Technical recommendations for psychological tests and diagnostic techniques. Psychological Bulletin, 51, 1-38.

American Psychological Association. (1992). Ethical principles of psychologists and code of conduct. *American Psychologist,* 47, 1597-1611.

ASTD (American Society for Training and Development) (2006). *Career planning and talent management. Module 9.* ASTD Press.

Aramburu-Zabala Higuera, L. (2001). Adverse impact in personnel selection: The legal framework and test bias. *European Psychologist,* 6(2), 103-111.

Barnett, Jeffrey, E. The complete practitioner: still a work In progress. *American Psychologist.* November 2009. (pp. 793-801). Barrick, M.R. & Mount, M.K. (1991). The big five personality dimensions and job performance: A meta-analysis. *Personnel Psychology,* 44,1-26.

Biddle. D. A., & Nooren, P. M. (2006). Validity generalization: Can employers successfully defend tests without conducting local validation studies? *Labor Law Journal.* 57(4), 216-237.

Block, P. (2011). *Flawless Consulting.* Wiley. San Francisco, CA.

Briner, R. B. and Rousseau, D. M. (2011), Evidence-based I-O psychology: Not there yet. *Industrial and Organizational Psychology,* 4: 3–22.

Broderick, P.C., & Blewitt, P. (2006). *The life span: Human development for helping professionals.* Upper Saddle River, NJ. Person Education Inc.

Blustein, D. L. (2008). The role of work in psychological health & well-being: A conceptual, historical, and public policy perspective. *American Psychologist,*63(4), 228-240.

Bucic, T., Robinson, L., & Ramburuth, p. (2010) Effects of leadership style on team learning. *Journal of WorkPlace Learning*, Vol . 22(4) 228-248.

Cascio, W. & Aguinis, H. (2011). *Applied psychology in human resource management.* Pearson, Upper Saddle River, New Jersey.

Cascio, W. F., & Ramos, R. A. (1986). Development and application of a new method for assessing job performance in behavioral/economic terms. *Journal Of Applied Psychology,* 71(1), 20-28.

Chamberlain, L., & Hodson, R.. (2010). Toxic work environments: What helps and what hurts. *Sociological Perspectives*, 53(4), 455-478.

Chase, Theodore (1972). Griggs v. Duke Power Company equal opportunity activity. *American Business Law Journal* (pre1986). 10 (1) p. 73.

Delprato, D. J., & Midgley, B. D. (1992). Some fundamentals of B. F.. Skinner's behaviorism. *American Psychologist*, 47(11), 15071520.

Equal Employment Opportunity Commission, Civil Service Commission, Department of Labor &Department of Justice. (1978) *Uniform guideline on employment selection procedures.* Washington, DC.

Figueroa, E. B., & Woods, R. A. (2007). Industry output and employment projections to 2016. *Monthly Labor Review,* 130(11), 53-85.

French, J.R.P., Caplan, R.D., & Harrison, R.V. (1982). *Mechanisms of job stress and strain.* New York. John Wiley.

Ford, G. G. (2006). *Ethical reasoning for mental health professionals.* Thousand Oaks, CA. Sage

Glasser, J. K. (2002). Factors related to consultant credibility. *Consulting. Psychology Journal,* Vol. 54,1, 28–42.

Graen, G. B., Liden, R. C., and Hoel, W. (1982). Role of leadership in the employee withdrawal process. *Journal of Applied Psychology,*67, 868-872.

Grant, A. M., & Cavanagh, M. J. (2007). Evidence-based coaching: Flourishing or languishing?. *Australian Psychologist, 42*(4), 239-254.

Gray, D. E., (2007) Facilitating management learning: developing critical reflection through reflective tools from management learning. *Management Learning.* Vol. 38, issue 5, pages 495–517.

Hays, P. A. (2008). *Looking into the clinician's mirror: Cultural self-assessment. In Addressing cultural complexities in practice: Assessment, diagnosis, and therapy* (2nd ed.) (pp. 41-62).

American Psychological Association.

Hunter, J.E. & Hunter, R.F. (1984). Validity and utility of alternative predictors of job performance. *Psychological Bulletin,* 96(1), 72-98.

Jaques, E. (2001). Diagnosing Sources of Managerial Leadership Problems for Research and Treatment. *Consulting Psychology Journal: Practice and Research.* 53(2) 67-75.

Jones, David P. (2011). *Million dollar hire.* San Francisco, CA. Jossey-Bass.

Kelleher, B. (2011). Engaged employees=High-performing organizations. In Article 5, *Human Resources.* Fred H. Maidment (Ed).

Kenner, C., & Weinerman, J. (2011). Adult learning theory: Applications to non-traditional college students. *Journal of College Reading and Learning, 41*(2), 87-96.

Koch, A. K., & Nafziger, J. (2011). Self-regulation through Goal Setting. Scandinavian *Journal Of Economics*, 113(1), 212-227

Kaplan, R.M. & Saccuzzo, D. P. (2009). *Psychological testing; Principles, applications and issues.* Wadsworth, Belmont, CA.

Kauffman, C. (2006). Chapter 8: *Positive psychology: The science at the heart of coaching.* In D. R. Stober, & A. M. Grant (Eds.), *Evidence based coaching handbook: Putting best practices to work for your clients* (pp.219-253). Hoboken, NJ: Wiley.

Landy, F.J., & Conte, J.M. (2010). *Work in the 21st century: An introduction to industrial and organizational psychology.* Hoboken, NJ; John Wiley & Sons, Inc.

Leedy, P. D., & Ormrod, J. E. (2013). *Practical research: Planning and design* (10th ed.). Upper Saddle River, NJ: Pearson.

Lombardo, Michael M; Eichinger, Robert W (1996). The career architect development planner (1st ed.). Minneapolis: Lominger

Luthans, F. & Peterson, S. (2002). Employee engagement and manager self-efficacy: Implications for managerial effectiveness and development. *Journal of Management Development.* Vol. 21(5).

Maister, D. H., Green, C. H., & Galford, R. M. (2000). *What is a trusted advisor? Consulting to Management,* 11(3), 36-41.

McClintock, Charles. (2003). Scholar Practitioner Model. *Encyclopedia of Distributed Learning.*

McIntire, S. A., & Miller, L. A. (2007). *Foundations of psychological testing: A practical approach (2nd ed).* Thousand Oaks, CA:Sage.

Norcross, J.C.,Gallegher, K.M., Prochaska, J.O., The boulder and/or vail model, training preferences of clinical psychologists. *Journal of Clinical Psychology.* 1989 September 45 (5) 822-8.

Northouse, P. G. (2010) *Leadership: Theory and practice.* Sage. Thousand Oakes, CA.

Palmer, H., & Valet, W. (2001). Job analysis: targeting needed skills. *Employment Relations Today.* Wiley. 28(3), 85-92.

Perloff, Robert. (2005). What lies ahead for I/O psychology and psychologist managers. *Psychologist-Manager Journal*, 8(1), 89-96.

Popper, M., and Mayseless, O. (2003) Back to basics: applying a parenting perspective to transformational leadership. *The Leadership Quarterly*, 14, 41-65.

Rath, T., & Conchie, B. (2008) *Strengths based leadership: Great leaders, teams, and why people follow them.* Gallup Press. New York, NY.

Reynolds, M. (2012). Reflection and critical reflection in management learning. *Management Learning.* Vol 29:2. 183-200.

Sackett, P.R., & Ellingson, J.E. (1997). The effects of forming multi-predictor composites on group differences and adverse impact. *Personnel Psychology*, 50, 707-721.

Schaffer, R. (1999). Replacing recommendations with results, new paradigm for consulting. *Consulting Psychology Journal Practice and Research.* Vol. 51, No. 4, 242-251.

Schaffer, R. (2002). High impact consulting: Achieving extraordinary results. *Consulting To Management.* Vol. 13, (2).

Schein, E. H. (1990). A general philosophy of helping: Process consultation. *Sloan Management Review*, 31(3), 57-57.

Schmidt, F.L. & Hunter, J.E. (1998). The validity and utility of selection methods in personnel psychology: Practical and theoretical implications of 85 years of research findings. *Psychological Bulletin*, 124, 262-274.

Scientist-Practitioner Versus Practitioner-Scholar. *The Counseling Psychologist.* 28. 622

Stober, D. R., & Grant, A. M. (2006). Introduction. In D. R. Stober, & A. M. Grant (Eds.), *Evidence based coaching handbook: Puttingbest practices to work for your clients* (pp.2-7). Hoboken, NJ: Wiley.

Swenson, L. E. (1997) *Psychology and the law (2nd edition).* Pacific Grove, CA. Brooks/Cole.

Tones, M., Pillay, H., & Kelly, K. (2011). The link between age, career goals, and adaptive development for work-related learning among local government employees. *Journal of Career Assessment* February 2011 19: 92.

Turner, S.M., Demers, S.T., Fox, H.R. & Reed, G.M. (2001). APA's guideline for test user qualifications: An executive summary. *American Psychologist*, 56, 1009-1113.

Vespia, K. M. Integrating professional identities: Counseling psychologist, scientist-practitioner and undergraduate educator. *Counseling Psychology Quarterly*, September 2006:19(3); 265-280.

Vosburgh, R. M. (2007). The evolution of HR: Developing HR as an internal consulting organization. *HR.Human Resource Planning*, 30(3), 11-16,18-23.

Wells, J. B. (2008). How rigorous should your training evaluation be? *Corrections Today*, 70(5), 116-118.

Yukl, G. (2006). *Leadership in organizations. (6th ed.).* Upper Saddle River, NJ: Pearson.

Zimmerman B.Z. & Schunk, D.H. (2003). *Educational Psychology: A Century of Contributions.* Routledge. New York, NY.